SYMPTOMS

POEMS WRITTEN BY A FRONTLINE MENTAL HEALTH WORKER DURING THE COVID 19 PANDEMIC

BY DAVID THOMAS

Dedicated to my Daughters Lilly and Sophia

Die alone
I'm not really afraid of dying alone
Actually I plan on it
Caskets aren't built for two
It's the living alone that scares me

The shopping alone
The eating alone
The sleeping alone
The turning to ask if I should buy this shirt and no one is there
That really haunts me
Dying alone is just fine
I don't want to take anyone with me
But I sure would love someone coming along for the ride

Zhivago
On a Russian train at seventeen I sat
Russian trains are cold and slow and passionless
No one smiles in Russia
It's against the rules
You're weird if you do
I bet they use to
I bet they use to smile and laugh and sing
And drink and make love till dawn to their soulmates
But shit happened as it always does to people
And they thought happiness is a dangerous thing
Fleeting like a fleas life
Better prepare for the worst
Constantly
And embrace stoic sadness religiously
No one smiles in Russia

Oh shit I forgot my mask
I'm sorry I know what this looks like
I'm just so tired
I keep forgetting to pay my bills too
My head is in a million places
I'm worried about my daughters
I'm worried about my clients
Most are in crisis
Fighting one's personal demons is one thing fighting another's is tricky and tiring
And you're all they have
I see your looks
I must be some kind of rebel
I'm not I'm just tired and worried
And oh shit I forgot my mask
And here is you're shining moment to feel virtuous and say something to me about it
You must be psychic you can know my character in a flash
You can just look at me and know my heart is corrupt and should be judged
Oh shit I forgot my mask
I promise I care
I'm just tired
Aren't you tired too?
I just want to be normal
Whatever that means now because I don't know
Oh shit I forgot my mask

Know my place
I know my place I always have
I guess I just really don't like it
I guess I just want more
I want to have more
And be more
Live more laugh more
It's shocking how all these years later
It's still high school
And I'm not at the cool kids table
Or the rich kids table
I'm at my little table
And the rich kids
And the cool kids are older but still at their table as well
Nothing really changes in this town
I wish it did
I tried
Now they say stay in your lane that's the lingo
But what they really mean is don't sit at my table you don't belong

I know my place I always have
I know my table where I use to sit
My daughters sit there now

Poems as weapons
Change and revolutions start with words
Not guns
Not bullets or bricks or swords
But words
Let my words infect you with the desire for change
Let my words cause you to want more
Let my words cause you to see more in the mirror
You should you know
You're way more than they say
Or those dark feelings that you feel

About yourself
Or the world
Don't let them make you hate yourself
Or think less of yourself
Cause you're truly more
Stand up
Stand up
Stand up
And say it
Say who you are and what you want
What you deserve
Let my words cause you to want more

Shuffle the deck
My hand is always the same
House wins you lose

Shuffle the deck
I know the odds are not in my favor
But still I play
Hoping
Believing
Losing hope
Clawing at the bottom of the jar for that one last shred of hope when hope is all gone and seems like bullshit
Shuffle the deck
I want a new hand
Can't be losing all the time
Right
This seat is hard and these pretzels are stale
You'd think you'd have better pretzels all my hope you take from me
Shuffle the deck
I want a new hand
It's the same hand every time I play

Cool like Colin Firth
My mouth gives me away I'm straight from the streets
I cuss like a sailor
And make stupid jokes that aren't funny
I'm loud and sometimes obnoxious and don't think before I speak
I wear high socks with shorts
And frumpy hats that make no sense
I try to be cool or suave
I try to dress the part
I have suits
Well 1 I think lots of ties
And a pair of dress shoes
Oh and a fake Rolex
Don't ask where I got it I won't tell
I wish I was cool like Colin Firth
And not so coarse not so street
He has a cool British accent
He could read a soup recipe
And command respect
I bought a cardigan last week
I look like I stole it from Mr. Rogers I think
I want to be cool like Colin Firth
I bet he always says the right things
And when he passes people believe his destiny is great
I doubt he uses toilet paper
I doubt he even shits
Or farts
Or makes mistakes
There I go again
My street is showing
I want to be cool like Colin Firth

It's raining
It's raining outside I can hear it
And that's ironic because it's raining in my heart as well
I'm so sad
And you're not allowed to say that when you're a man cause we're not
allowed to be sad it's the rules
Whose rules I don't know
Boy it's really coming down
I hear it trickling against my roof
And invading my porch
Boy I'm really sad
And worried
And hoping all this madness will be over one day
I worry about my daughters
1 is tough
And 1 is not
I just want them to be okay
Boy I'm really sad
Can you believe I'm saying that out loud?
There must be something wrong with me
All this brutal honesty
It's just not normal
Wear a mask so to speak
It will protect you so to speak

People will judge you and think you're weak
You can feel bad all you want
Just don't say it out loud
Boy I'm really sad

Breakfast at Tiffany's

I can't afford what they have but I like to look
Maybe one day I say to myself
Maybe one day
When my ship comes in and I'm covered in money
And my bank account is full and ready to vomit cash

Then I'll buy that thing I've always seen that I know will make me
happy
But to be honest if my ship doesn't come in
It's okay

Because every time I have Breakfast at Tiffany's
You're there with me
Having breakfast and starving too
It's a cold crisp morning as we walk away
I stop you and tighten your coat
Like a jeweler wrapping a stone
Because I know
I don't want breakfast with anyone else
And things are just things

That's not Santa
It's Christmas Eve
And I'm snuggled up on the couch warm in cheek
The year is almost over and lethal weapon 1 rocks me to sleep
Suddenly I awake at a familiar sound
What's this?
It can't be
It's the sound of my ex-wife's laughter in the house as I sleep
Oh shit I say
As I spring for a leap
I grab my heart and checkbook
And toss them in the basement
She'll never go there
Louder and louder her laughter becomes
I military crawl thru the living room to the kitchen
Help me Bing Crosby
Help me Johnny Mathis
Help me lieutenant Riggs from lethal weapon
What shall I do?

I'll just hide behind the refrigerator and drink this beer
Merry Christmas to all
And to all a good night

Human for once
I want to kidnap you with nerf guns and ski masks
And chase each other on the trails by your house
Till we're winded and need an ambulance and maybe some Ben gay
I pull shit so easily nowadays
And running sounds a bit much
Would you have fun I wonder
Shooting me with foam darts and screaming and forgetting this shit year
we've had
I'm sorry about your year
That had to be tough

I offer you watered down violence
And drinking in the end
Oh and my best body part
My ears
They work amazing
I can listen for days
Maybe together we could be
Human for once

Siberia
I'm Guilty of something

I'm not sure what it is
Everyone else seems to know my crime except me
Alone feels right
I think it's my sentence
Not sure when I get out
I try to escape all the time
It starts with a smile or a text
And I think this may be my parole but it's not it never is
When I was 17 I got a new name and thought briefly I found my dream
a family of my own
I was wrong
When I was 25 I got married I thought I found the love of my life
I was wrong
Been wrong with friends
Been wrong with love
My heart is as cold as ice now
My soul lives in Siberia

Strait jacket
I use to be a magician
When I was younger
I use to escape from strait jackets
Real ones actually
There's no trick
You have to be calm
Not panic and slowly think your way out
I could do it in a minute
I was very proud of that
I did the 100 foot rope escape as well
A farmer tied me to a chair
I got out
I am great at escaping
Really
But I can't escape you
I try to let you go
Get mad at you
Go another way
I always like a compass come back to north
You're my north
So to speak
My heart twists and squirms and wriggles
But I'm so stuck
And embarrassed because the crowd is watching
And they paid for a show
And here I am an escape artist
Who can't escape?
How embarrassing
Your picture sits on my chair
By my bed
I know the prison you're in
I was in 1 too

I served 17 years
I thought I was going to die there
I finally escaped
Some wardens are just cruel
And want you to pay for everything that ever happened to them
I don't think you're like that
If I'm ever caught in your cage
I'll gladly wear orange
And never try to escape

Dear Tammi
I miss you first and foremost
You were a mother to my daughter Sophia
For that I am ever grateful
I never lost anyone before
The night my coworker called to tell me I collapsed on the dining room
floor and sobbed like a baby for hours
I couldn't stand up
But I could slither
I slithered into the corner of my dining room and I froze
How do I tell Sophia?
She has never lost anyone either
How do I tell my daughter that the woman who stood up and filled the
position of mom to her was gone?
Death is like a song in your head that you love and can't replace the cd
or cassette
It embers in your memory and to touch the breath of the song you have
to stir the memories in your mind
The cruelty is that's all you get
Are memories
I just talked to you the day before
We were going to the zoo with the girls
That was the plan

How do you know?
How do you know?
That you are real
Or alive
Or touching God
It's your love that makes you real
It's your love that makes you whole
Your ability to slip on the soul shoes of another and sit awhile and listen
God is not a book or a building
Or a weapon to make your ego feel superior to another
Or a title that makes people acknowledge you in the grocery store
God is a verb
Action
Connection
And kindness

Snarling lusts for Lear jets
And expensive suits
And bigger pulpits
Makes God cry
Loving the least makes you the most
Can't you see?
Love someone
Open your heart to those the world tells you to shun
To despise
To ignore
To neglect

Boxing gloves
Get in the ring with me
Put on those boxing gloves
Sharpen my character with your intellect
I trust you
Hell I adore you
I always have
My edges are rough and raw

I need someone like you
To help me be a better man
There is so much for me to learn
I want to be your student
I won't leave the ring
That's for cowards
I know a worthy opponent I've waited my whole life
I'll even hold your spit bucket as we spar
And grow and become
Who we are supposed to be
To beat this world
Which spars us all

Archangel
I see your armor
You're not fooling me
You don't even know you're wearing it
You think that's just who you are
The arrows of life harden us
Make us see smiling as dangerous
And hope as foolishness
And love as an impossibility
I see your armor and it doesn't scare me
I once wore armor too
And I thought that that was me
And I wore it proudly
My anger coursing thru my veins like fire
I was full of arrows
I wasn't going to love anymore
Oh no not me
I'm above that
Everyone's wearing armor now
And full of hate and judgement and pain
Hearts were set afire long before any buildings
Look at us now with our armor
Look at us now with our hate
I won't drink it
I won't go back
You can go to hell
I won't
I just got out
I just got free
I will smile till my teeth fall out
I will love no matter who mocks me or spits in my face or calls me
names
I won't go back
Hell isn't hot
Oh no that's a myth
Hell is armor that separates you from your brother your sister the family
at large
I won't go back

Wonder Woman
I wonder what makes you happy
I wonder if I could get into your heart
I wonder what you think of me
I wonder if you know how awesome you are
I wonder if you know that it killed me to see you cry
I wonder if I'll see you again
Or if you think I'm too strange too odd
And should be medicated and watched closely
You're probably right
There's no advantage to sanity right now
The heart is my boss
I wonder if you'll read this
I hope you do
I wonder if you'll pause for a moment and smile
Even a half smile no one has to know
That you are my Wonder Woman

Can't come home
I'm sorry but you can't come home
You lived here for many years but you never really were here
You were always somewhere else and with someone else
It's a small town
Everyone knew
I was your clown
I was your fool
I was your beast of burden
You're free now
Time to be an adult
I don't envy you
You had someone who loved you
And you didn't see it
You had someone who adored you and you didn't care
You must be scared
The world is dark and cruel and loveless
Digging in the dirt for diamonds with no lights
Is it a rock?
Or is it a diamond
You'll never know
I don't envy you

Please stop asking
Because you can't come home

Smallville
Martha and Clark Kent didn't like the orphan they found
I'm sorry I was so different
I'm sorry I wasn't good enough
I'm sorry I can fly
I'm nothing like you
You didn't want me in your nest with the rest of your birds
I looked awkward and was clumsy and fell out
You took me to a dark place

I never want to go back
You took family pictures and forgot my last name
I needed you to forget you found me and pretend that I was really yours
The other birds got all the worms
My plate was always empty
You're on Gods side you say
I don't see it
My daughters are from krypton too
You wouldn't let them in you didn't care
It's easy to leave you
I always come back
That's what orphans do
You say it will be different it never is
It was my dream to be a son
To have a home
I thought I won for once
But I was wrong

Botox my heart
Botox my heart
Is that a thing?
Can someone turn back the clock on my heart?
It's old
And cold
And doesn't believe anymore

When I jump up and down
You can hear the shattered pieces of it rattling around
It's embarrassing
Sometimes pieces tend to fall out all over
I virtually don't know how much is left
Am I fixable?
Please please
I don't want to hear about your pyramid scheme
I'm not going to give you my credit card number
I'm not going to sign anything
Screw your dotted line
I used to sing as a kid
I want to go back there
I used to dream as a kid that would be nice
To go back too

Don't waste your time
On love never returned
Or trying to win people
Who aren't worth winning
You don't have to do all that
Don't waste your time
It's priceless
God doesn't stand on the street corner peddling more time
It's accounted for already
There's an end
Drink it up
Laugh all you want
Watch that sunset longer
Be strange
Be weird
Scare the Gods
Open your door to someone
If they don't come in
Keep trucking
Drink that beer
Listen to that song
Smile
While you have teeth
Run while you have feet
Do everything that scares you
Don't listen to your angels
They wish they were you anyway
Don't waste your time
It's quick
One day you'll look back
At every year, month, week, day, hour, and second you wasted on
assholes and foolishness
And you will weep
Don't waste your time

Find a way
We're trapped and prisoners
And afraid
But find a way
Find a way to love
Find a way to heal and breathe
Find a way to be alive
Find a way to grieve
Make it your own
You can do it
Sing somehow like my mother Maya Angelou would say
Find a way
Don't be stifled
Don't give up
Find a way
Pull that old heart out of your chest
Dust it off
Lift it up like John Cusack did his boom box in that movie where he
wins the girl in the end by proclaiming his love
Find a way
Be your most human
Be divine
And above all this hate
And darkness
And bitterness
Don't drink from that cup anymore
We can change this
We can overcome
Find a way

Eat slowly
I chew slowly and have a romantic relationship with every bite
Like a man on death row
Who knows he's not going to be pardoned
Taste those eggs
Savor the butter spread on the toast
Slowly sip that coffee
With the perfect amount of cream and sugar
In an old man's coffee cup
Do everything slowly and as if I'll never do it again
Because life is unpredictable on the one hand and predictably short and
surprising on the other
Walk slow
Look at birds as if you've never seen one before
Hold hands like they're one hand and not two
Love slowly
Every moment is sacred
Smile at it
This is all there is

The girl in the red wool coat

I see your Joan of arc armor
And I want more
I've seen you're tears
You can't stuff them all back in
it's too late
I know you're not a dragon

Let me sharpen your sword
Polish your armor
Hell I'll even feed your horse
I won't be a bother or nuisance
I know your fight
It's mine too
I just want to listen
Forever if you like

You think I'm crazy
And I'm sure your right
Judge me not with your mind
That's jaded and beaten by life
Let your heart feel my cause
I kneel before you
I deserved judged and harshly
I am deficient and laughable and weak and a fool
No one throws stones at me like I do
here you go take this brick
It's not as heavy
As my thoughts for you

Sabrina
I'm more Humphrey than Harrison

I'm shorter than you
You've always been tall in my book
Since the first time I saw you on the field in high school
Save me from my bow tie and brief case
Run away to Paris with me
This isn't who we are
This isn't living
Be my Sabrina
I need this
I think you need it too
Let's drink lattes and talk shit about our abyss of a town
Save me from this
My bow tie is choking me
And my brief case is too heavy
I smiled at you in court that day
Because it was you
I was weeping before and scared and fighting for my kids
And there you were
My favorite person
So I smiled
Because I was happy
And you walked on by
Run away with me

2021
I want to hope and believe like the scariest blind date that this is going
to be better
I'm tired of masks
And hate and politics
I want more
I want a better life
An endless cup of coffee
The sun to always shine on my face
A bank account that comforts me like a warm blanket
I'm tired of all this class
And poverty and fighting and racism
I want to drink wine
And lay with you on a boat
A boat
Yes
A boat
That's how rich in life I want to be
I can flee this land
And make my home the sea
Will you bring relief 2021?
Or increase humanity's grief
Will things really change?
Can we rise from this?
Will people stop dying?
Can we breathe?
Can Halloween Cease?
Can we touch each other and not be afraid
Or worried
Can I show my teeth?
Can I smile?
2021
State your purpose before knocking on my door
You're not coming in unless you're better
What do you have to offer?
I need more

I need better
I need that
We need that
I'm so tired
This isn't living
Take this mad max, I am legend, and George Orwell shit and shove it
I want to be free
I want to breathe and live second by second
We all do
Will you love us 2021?
Will you treat us right?

To the lonesome losers of the world
You are awesome
And it's cool that you don't fit
Would you really want to anyway?
Just saying
That sadness you carry
That pain of not belonging to the herd
Is wasted
They don't deserve you
To the lonesome losers of the world
Rejoice you're better than what you get
Another attempt at love and joining failed
Oh well they weren't for you
They'll go back to their kind and say you aren't right
And it's true
You're not like them
To the lonesome losers of the world
One day
One day
You'll not be thinking about what a lonesome loser you are and you'll
walk in a room and you'll lock eyes with someone
Lonesome loser and you won't be lonesome anymore

The hermit
Take a break from the world
Heal and go inside yourself to reflect and learn
The world will be there when you return don't worry
We get blinded and blindsided by the noise of the world
We get confused by the lies that we're told
We're only human
Step away from all that
Let your heart do the talking and sort out the mess
Still waters clear faster and you can see the bottom
Listen to yourself
That heart voice
Do what it says
Not all those loud crazy voices around you
Be a hermit for a while
It's not forever
It's just a phase

Stayed too long
I stay too long
You ever do that
I stick around for years
When the love is gone

Or lie to myself that love is there to begin with
I wait with orphan eyes
And I put them on a pedestal in the kingdom of my mind
But to them I'm nothing
And it's shocking to see the years you've clutched at a belief wasted
It's like getting hit with a can of tea so to speak
But I needed it
I'm getting old and time is more ruthless and short
Don't be like me
Don't stay too long
Don't beg and wait to be loved or accepted
Don't put someone on a pedestal who belongs in a sewer
Time is ticking
Love yourself
Enough to go
And never go back
Never go back

I'm awake today
It's the first
First for everything actually
First day of hope and expectation
When I wake up my first thought is getting this cat off of my head
My second thought is coffee
I'm off today
But I'm not
Lots to write about for the work I've done this week
I have a half good feeling about this year
Yesterday was shitty and I drank alone
I'm a regular George thorogood so to speak
As I write I worry
I worry about businesses and the economy
And children
And people not coping
I worry about the next three months
And how they'll fare
My soul is quiet
Today
I said goodbye to the past
Poured gas on that bridge and lit it up
The streets are quiet
Is everyone like me?
Wondering if the day is safe
And brings promise
I understand now why Bukowski drank fear runs away
And words appear
I don't know how to end this poem
I truly don't
How do you quietly scream when you lost your voice?

Pillar of salt
Don't do the same thing
Be different
Change
Don't put up with the same bullshit
Or operate the same way
Be different
No more fake ass friends
No more fake ass family
No more begging to be loved
Be different
Stop caring what others think
It doesn't matter anyway
Here's a thought
Love yourself
You're always loving others
Why not love yourself
For a change
You deserve to be loved start with you
You do so much for others
Do for you
You've got a whole new year
Don't do the same thing
Or think the same nasty thoughts about yourself
They aren't true
Recreate yourself
Recreate your life
Be someone different
Don't look back

The judges
Crocodiles are interesting until you get close
Then you're in trouble
They sit on their thrones
And toss out labels on others
Your throne is up high
Above the clouds even
I'm so short and can't reach
I'm
Close to the ground
I apologize for that
No tell me more
Show me your list of what's wrong with me
Please do tell
I know I know you represent the light
Then why are you so dark
Do you even know?
Did you break your mirrors?
I would if I were you
Your number 2 must smell like Chanel number 5
So glad to meet you
Thank you for allowing me to breathe the same oxygen as you for a bit

Do I owe you anything?
Does it get lonely?
Judging others and chomping down on people like that
Your horse is high I could never afford one
What's that like really
God must be thankful you're doing his job
Giving him a break

My anti balding regimen
I'm not keeping up with the kardashians
That shit is fake
I have wrinkles and crow's feet
I can't touch my toes and I look like I'm stealing a bag of candy under
my shirt
I'm aging and not gracefully
My skin is patchy
Sometimes dry
But here I am
Oh and like my wife my hair left me a long time ago
But I love it
I wouldn't want it any other way

Vikings wore scars and blemishes like medals
Who wants to be pretty?
Or handsome
Or have manicured hands that have never experienced dirt
I don't
When I go home I want to look like I did 12 rounds with Tyson
Don't fix me up funeral director
Don't erase time or its effects
I want to go like a well-worn trusted coat
With missing buttons and a hole in the pocket
I don't want people to say I aged well
I want people to say that guy fought hard and lived and drank and loved
and stood up against assholes
And tried to do good and he's got the scars to prove it

Kicked out of heaven
I'm not allowed back in I guess
I'm not good enough for you

Or them or anyone I guess
I've lived in heaven in my mind on earth
And in my mind's eye you're my queen
And you love me and all is right with the world
But I pinch myself reality check
You still love the law
Well good for you Red Queen
Sorry I'm so fallen
I can't get this hades off my skin
And I still have my wings
And this halo that I hate
It's cumbersome and gets in the way of my hat
And sleeping with these wings and halo is a total pain in the ass I swear
How do I shed this skin?
Is there another planet I can go to?
Ticket please
Where's the bus
I want to let go
Any thoughts of us

Heathcliff
It's the quiet times that I hate the most
Your ghost comes home and haunts me to no end
Orphans never fare well with love
We had a shitty start
We play Marco Polo with love our entire lives
Not shocking we never find love
We don't know what it is
If it bit us like a shark
We'd think it was something else
Nice flea bite we'd say
And then we'd thank the shark and wish it well
That's an orphan for you
If you want to know my dowry
It's all in my eyes
See that fire
That's all for you
I'm filled with fire
And my empty heart
My empty life
My empty soul long for you
Your rejection has made me cruel
And dark
But I still wait like a gargoyle
On your step
I am stone
But you can change that
If you want

Cool like Dracula
I wish I was cool like Dracula
He's a great dresser
And has a title
I bet you'd like me then
I wish I was cool like Dracula
With hypnotic eyes that put you under my spell
And you'd want to live in my castle forever
I wish I was cool like Dracula
He lives in a castle
I live in a house on Milner with my daughter
We had a bat once
I let it out
Bats are cool on TV in real life not so much
I wish I was cool like Dracula
He doesn't seem to care
About anything or anyone really
Me I haven't slept in weeks
And he sleeps in a coffin
But my ocd would go crazy and I'd be afraid of someone accidentally
locking me in
I wish I was cool like Dracula
He'd walk right up to you
I could never do that

You'd think I was crazy or asking for directions
Or lost and I am
I wish I was cool like Dracula
He's been alone for a very long time
And he's cool with that
I'm not though it kind of sucks
When you're alive
To live like you're dead
I wish I was cool like Dracula

Baptism
I am fat with love
The bread is thick
The wine sweet and red
Baptize me in your soul
My communion wafer is you
And every day is Sunday
Forget drinking bath water
That's totally gross
Hymns fill my heart every day for you
I am your sinner
Save me
Be my altar
I sacrifice my past to you
Make me anew

I want to be worthy of you
I'll never have a halo
I'll never have wings
But I will Fashion wings out of feathers
And put a flashlight behind my head
If I can find heaven with you

How to heal from what ails you
If you heart is troubled and filled with pain
And your feet are heavy
And blistered by life
You got to let it all out to go forward
Speak your truth

Share your pain
With a guide or mentor or friend
Who will listen to your story?
Who will listen to your pain?
Who will stay with you during your grief?
Who will sponge away the sweat from your brow?
And be unmoving like a stoic statue
Find a doctor for your soul
An Angel for your heart
And sit with them
Take what's inside of you
And do something with it
Take that darkness
And make it light
Write
Dance
Sing
Create
You're a creator like your creator
And you're happiest when you're doing so
Dance with the divine within
That's where God lives
Not in a fancy church
Or book
But in your heart
Go there
Go there
Go there
Read books about healing
Look in the mirror stop believing the world's lies
You're not what you think
You're so much more
Expect love
Expect love
Expect love
And don't try to eat from an empty plate
You don't need to do that anymore
Dream
You're allowed
Heal and become this for someone else

Be a doctor for their soul

Clown make up
Is it just me, or is it getting crazier out there?
That line is so true now
In the 80s the joker was dropped in a vat of liquids to be transformed
Today cruel society does the job of transforming
Him
How do I not be transformed like it says in the Bible?
How do I still believe in love?
The air is thick with death and fear
Shopping at Walmart is hard
Even though we're all wearing masks
Our fear and worry about our lives is still very readable on each face
We're all trapped hamsters
Hoping for some last ditch semblance of connection
We claw at our cages
We run our metal cups across the bars
Back and forth
Please someone
Make this stop
I just want it to be over
I want to smile
I do
And laugh
I've had tastes of humanity during all of this
But they're very fleeting and cold quickly like leftovers that I'll never
eat

New Year feels
New Year feels well the same like last year
I lie to myself sometimes and say it'll be a different movie
When in fact it's the same movie
So to speak
And shockingly so
I say that allot
In my imaginary fights with you
I want to be hopeful
That keeps me afloat
I'm afraid of drowning
I thought you were my boat
Oops wrong again
Why do my future hopes
Always become my past regrets

I don't need a belt anymore
I've reached that middle aged milestone
Where I don't need a belt to hold up my pants anymore
I'm like low budget Santa
I remember when I was young and wore slim jeans
Those days are gone
Thanks to pizzas and chocolate glazed donuts
And aging
And rivers of iced coffee
I could diet
I could work out more
I could plank for hours
But then I'd have to get new pants
But then I'd need a belt
And I don't miss my old one
Honestly I blame McDonald's
Maybe I should sue
Those Golden Arches are just so easy

I'm torn by ideas of what I should look like and who I realistically am
The big thing is looking good naked I guess
Cause you'll die alone if you don't
But then again
At least I won't go hungry

Snoring in my sleep
I snore in my sleep
My mouth is open like a crocodile in mid chomp
The noise and I can attest because I've actually woken myself up is
pretty intolerable to most humans but seems to be music to you
You never take the couch which is shocking
You've never left for anything
Not even at your maddest
Or saddest which I'm guilty of causing you

When I'm a stubborn bastard
And I am
Love isn't pretty or sexy
In the beginning it is
When skin is soft and new
But that's the trick
That's the lure
Real love comes much later
When teeth fall out
And demons appear
And jobs are lost
And the nakedness of our imperfections show
Stretch marks and all
You never have left not even once
That's that old school kind of love
Noah Calhoun yelling what do you want kind of love
I'm writing this poem in James garners voice as we speak I can't help it
Love makes you crazy
There is nothing sane about planting your flag of hope on the heart of
another human being
And never leaving them kind of love

The sins of my youth
I will tell you my sin
It haunts me to this day
Welcome to the abyss of my soul
My season In Hell
Occurred In my youth
I did not have a good start
My mom was ill in mind
My father was ill in heart
They couldn't do their job
So at 11 I was orphaned
With no shelter or love to speak
I grew up in a dark world
Full of violence and lack
I stole to survive
I lied to survive
I conned to survive
Yes I confess it to you my priest or priestess whatever your gender
I was an animal and lived like one
I taught myself to read
And my world changed
Frederick Douglas became my hero
A slave who taught himself to read as well
My light was always books
My world was always dark
I slept on roof tops
I slept in greyhound bus stations
I slept in garbage cans
I stole clothes from donation piles
This is my sin
My hair was long and matted
My skin dirty and ragged
My nails long
I was an animal
I lived like one
I thought like one
This is my sin
Here is a stone
I won't run

Cast it
Nothing transforms the heart like love
I went to a church for bread and found my humanity
Someone looked me in the eye as if I was human
They asked my name as if that was important
And the animal I was
Was no more

Acrylic Jesus
Where are you God
Hearts are stopping
And lungs can't breathe
And it's illegal to have black skin
Where are you God
In all of this
Everyone wants to fight
Hearts and minds are troubled
We can't sleep
Your children
Can you hear me God?
We need you
Where is the healer
Where is the prophet
Please roll the stone away from my heart
Show yourself God
We need you
I'm looking everywhere
I see an Osteen snake selling your love
Making you turn tricks
That isn't you
You stood for the poor
You healed the sick
You raised the dead
You loved the stranger
You parted seas to free the enslaved
Your silence is deafening and loud
Will he come with fiery eyes?
And hands on fire

And free us all
Will he speak truths out loud that frees our heart?
Will his gaze pierce our souls?
Will angels count his steps?
The churches are cold and the doors are locked
Where are you God

Venus and Mars
It's very French to have an affair
It's very American to be caught
We're always at war with each other
The sexes
There's no escaping the dance of Mars and Venus
It's actually more of an arm wrestling match than a dance
Does the devil disguise himself and attend church
Sometimes
Do the hymns make him cry?
Does he miss God?
Miss heaven
Does he ever toy with the idea of repenting?
I don't desire to be king
But for the right queen I'd be the grandest court jester ever
I'd do whatever it took to make her smile
I'd fall and feign great pain
I'd dress like a clown
And dance to close my eyes and hear her laugh
Let women rule for a change
We need them now

We've made the world our toilet and the rivers flow with blood
Give her the crown
She will rule with her heart
And the earth will be whole

Dry mouth
My lips are dry
And my throat is a desert
Maybe you'll change your mind about me
That's the orphan in me talking
No one can hear me in this mask
When I speak
I'm soft spoken
I think
This mask muzzles me
I think

I feel like a dog who bites and is muzzled
I shouldn't bitch
I've worn a mask all of my life
Never been honest about who I am
Or how I feel
Wore a mask to keep the peace
Don't ask for more Oliver know your place boy
She's not your kind
And by kind I mean class
Know your place boy
Your class is that way
You can look this way and dream and want
But the girl in the red wool coat will never belong to you
Wear your mask
No entrance if you don't
6 feet
6 feet
Not 3
Not 4
Not 5
6 feet
Keep your distance
Boy
Or you'll die

Ticket to Mars

Does your gun shoot love

I've never ate at that restaurant
I'm sure it's nice
Who is my neighbor
And what is this love thing
I need carpentry lessons
If I'm going to build an ark
It's for everyone
My ark
I legit love everyone
Black
White
Brown
Gay
straight
Trans
Come aboard
Come as you are
My father doesn't have mansions but he did make us all cool
apartments to live in
We have to share the laundry
Though
It's not the hotel California so to speak
Mother Abigail lives here

Bat Country
Welcome to bat country
Please read this in Johnny Depp's drunken voice
It'll all make sense
Oh and drink a little first
Might I recommend vodka?
The Russians swear by it
Dr gonzo was right
This is not a kid's show
I wouldn't want them watching this
Bats everywhere
And hate
And no shame
I don't care about the golf shoes
I'm not here to play golf
Look at those crocodiles storming the castle
She died
One of them
Was she a mother?
A wife
What do u tell her kids?
What about her husband
She's gone now you know forever
There is no sequel when you stop breathing
What about her children I say louder
And slightly more sober
What about our children
Maybe Joel Osteen with his magic teeth could buy them a flying carpet
Kids are watching this
Quick change the channel

Gray
I wear gray all the time now
In college I wore black
And listened to Marilyn Manson
And hated the world and anyone who smiled
I'm older now much older
And I know how to smile
I just can't
I try
Everything is so gray
The sun is on vacation
And so is love and human decency
I can't remember if today is Wednesday or Thursday
This happens allot
Bills I pay them when I remember and that's not allot
They sit in stacks on my table
All I can think about is Sophia and Lilly
I don't want them to wear black or gray
I don't want them to be like me
Sad or worried 24 7
And trying to change a world that isn't interested
When I go to sleep at night about the tenth time I wake up before dawn
I wonder
Will today be gray?

Bar fly
I meet allot of magicians in bars
They make their wedding rings disappear very quickly
But their fake tan
Reveals their even faker hearts
And goal of sin
And bullshitery
I know I know he was horrible
You deserve so much better
You're so noble and virtuous
It was all him
I'm sure of it
What a monster he was
What a total full of shit Saint you are
Humans are a dance all of us of God and the Devil within
When you try to tell me your only one

I know you're fully the other
My blue jeans have holes in them
My ashtray is full
And my breath
Smells like coffee
Mistakes and screw ups
I'll point the finger squarely at myself
I'm not looking for any scapegoat
My sin is my own
The goat can stay
You may leave

Doors
Doors are mysterious
You don't know what's behind a door that's not yours unless someone
on the other side lets you in
You can knock and if they don't open you never get to know
Never

And if someone knocks on your door
And you don't open
They remain ignorant of your secret truth as well
What's inside?
That's what counts
Doors protect us
Doors stop us
The doors we have keys to because their our doors we're good
It's the doors that aren't ours
Do you knock loud?
Do you soft knock?
Or knock in a friendly toned pattern
Yell it's me
It's cool you can open up
Unlock your door
Let me in I'll be safe
You won't be sorry
I'm dying to know
The truth of what's inside
Doors

Monsters
Sometimes the monsters aren't under our beds
Sometimes they are in them with us
Why do we choose horrible people to love?
Are we desperate and alone?
Is the alcohol too strong?
Like a convincing demon
Or do we just want what's bad for us sometimes
Yes that's the question
Do you sometimes pick people subconsciously who will tear your life apart?
I think so
How do u stop?
How do you wake up?
How do you never do that again?
Never let someone in your life who will ruin it
Never waste another second
With someone whose goal isn't love
At our core
And we complain
And criticize the demons we've been with
What I wonder is at my core
Opening the heart of my Pandora's Box
I secretly think I'm shit and deserve all that
And run to the flame like a stupid moth
I'm sobering up now
With age
And gray hairs in my beard
And I don't want the next half of my story to have any monsters

American Gods
It's a war I tell you a war
Odin is here and he wants the capitol
I know the Gods when I see them
And Odin wants Washington all to himself
His vision is singular
He only has one eye
It's us vs them
I see Christ
She's a nurse on a Covid unit in an overbooked hospital
This is all fiction this shit isn't real
Right
Where the hell is Zeus?
There's Mary
I see her full of grace and wiping mace from someone's eyes
She does that sort of thing you know
Always taking care of people
That's why God chose her
Hear those war drums
People die when they are played
See you in Valhalla
They say
Send me a postcard
I say
Buddha's in the library
People watching

Angels are all over
And they are scared
Scared for us
That it's too late
We won't get it
You know that big idea of loving one another
And not like a Carpenter song but for real
For real
Before it's too late
Where is Cupid
Work your magick
Make us all love each other as we should
Make all those ego illusions of race, politics and class disappear

Plates
Take a plate and raise it over your head as high as you can
Now throw it on the ground and watch it shatter into a million pieces
Now apologize to it
Say you're sorry
Does the plate Harry Potter style magically reverse your actions or is it
still broken
You feel better though I'm sure
And that's what counts right
Right
The weight of human actions is so heavy and deep
And carries reverberating consequences that can effect generations of
people
Yet we skip thru life sometimes haphazardly and
Like a bull in a China shop
We do the craziest shit because we feel like it
And when it's over

When the dust settles
And all of the dishes are broken the tea sets smashed we go to our
Sunday school training
And say
Sorry
Instead of taking the extra human effort to weigh our actions before
they're
Done
Sorry does nothing
But say how lazy you are at being a connected human
And thinking before you leap
You piss in the dark
As if there's no tomorrow
Or you're playing monopoly
And have a get out of jail free card
For life

Love is illegal now
I think things like love
And hope
And empathy

Should me made illegal
We should all be hating heartless robots because that's where we're
going
Once something is illegal or forbidden
Then we want to do it
Then we chase it like the coyote chases the roadrunner
Make love illegal
And people will fight for it
Make hope illegal
And people will believe
Make empathy and caring illegal
And people will face death to become one
Aren't we funny?
The things we chase
And the things that repel us
Make love, hope and empathy a forbidden fruit
It's against the law
And tap your index finger vigorously on a law book while saying it
The law
Love is forbidden
Hope is forbidden
Empathy is against the rules
Do that
And watch
All the apples start to be devoured
And hearts changed
Like dickens scrooge character
Watch the world change
Make love illegal

Unfriend
Unfriend
Block
Mute
I don't want to be your Facebook friend anymore
I don't want to see your life flash before my eyes no more
I'm done
Not that we were actually friends in the first place
Cause if I saw you in person I wouldn't say hi
So yeah
But occasionally I'll peep and see what you're doing
Or press a half ass like
But honestly
Sincerely
None of this is real
None of it
99% of the people you are so called friends with
Aren't really your friends
That's a borrowed word
Close your eyes picture what real friendship is
Does that look like what's happening on Facebook?
Definitely not
This isn't real
This is marketing
And we're all just consumers and products
And dollar signs to Zuckerberg
This isn't real
This isn't connecting
This is collecting
This is infecting
And this is dissecting normal healthy relationships
And making them disposable and cheap and a commodity
Do you really think you can push a button and disconnect from
someone

We're not robots
We're human beings
This isn't real
This is porn
And I'm no star
Look how easy it is to hate on Facebook
It's safe and sanitary
Like the person pulling the switch on the electric chair
And you can throw someone away when you're done the next day like a
Christmas tree
This isn't real

Dwight Yoakam
Guitars
Cadillac's
I don't have either
But I always have a broken heart
That is not in short supply
I'm old school country
Garth
Clint
George
And Dwight
They get it
Beer poetry
And blisters on my hands
And blisters on my heart
I love being on a horse
And taking off
I'm Steve McQueen in my mind
I look more like yul Bryner
The cowboy is always trying to find peace
Love eludes him like a fearful snake
In the grass
It's a solitary life he's done something in his brain that says he doesn't
deserve miss kitty

So he doesn't stay
I have no idea who Kane brown is
Or Luke Bryan
It's not that I don't believe them
Well yeah I don't believe them
I don't think their hearts have been smashed by the prettiest girl in the
county
Nor do I think they've ever smelled a horse let alone ride one or clean
its stall
Or been thrown
Cowboys know
You get thrown
And it can happen any time
You can think your horse is your best friend
And surprise she throws you and keeps going
I use to wear a cowboy hat when I was young
It was black
But then my heart was purer
It matches my hat now
This rodeo has been a long one
I've become that old cowboy cutting an apple
And philosophizing why my life didn't work out the way it should
And telling deaf young cowboys don't be like me
They humor me
Cause that's the rules
I'm going to have a beer now
And listen to Dwight yoakam
And think about your face
And what you looked like before it was over

Texting exes
I must be lonely
Cause here I go again

Texting you saying hi
I should stop I know
I make no sense
I ended it in fact I usually do
Are you there?
Do you miss me?
Are you lonely as hell too?
I'm not even drinking
Just intoxicated by sadness and loneliness and the sneaking suspicion I
wasn't made for anyone
I should stop
I'm so stupid
You're probably with someone
And it's meant to be
And working out
I'm always trying to cross bridges I've set fire too
I don't know why

Slow burn
You hang your head low
As you sip your coffee and bang away on that keyboard that pays your
bills
You feel that ember in your soul
You're older now
Getting out of bed is a chore
You just want to curl up into a ball and give up
Don't
Fuck that
Remember that ember you felt
It's you
That fire
That is your soul
Grab it and don't let go
It isn't over yet
Not by a long shot
Grab that fire and blow on it until the embers light
Let that fire consume your whole body
Your whole being
Your whole soul
Until you are a walking torch
Untouchable by the crap around you
Burn
Burn
Burn
Let that fire you hide come out
Light the way for others who hide their fire
Out of fear
Or exhaustion
Burn
Burn
Burn
Be the person you've always wanted to be
But we're afraid to

Eat, pray, love yourself
Only here once unless the Hindus are right
Every second is sacred
And no joke
And could be your last
Eat that steak
Chew it slowly as if it's your last
Have that cheese cake
Don't sin in moderation
Sin abundantly and slowly
Have fudge on it too
Oh and did I mention the fries
Have those as well
Talk
Talk
Talk
To God
Open your heart like a well-worn book
Pray for yourself
Ask for Advice and guidance
Pray for others
Be led by spirit
Be a walking altar for the divine
Sing

Sing
Sing
As you dance with the fire that is God
Love yourself
Shed the past like a snake does its skin
You're a living breathing temple of the divine
Yet you treat yourself like a filthy brothel
See yourself as you really are
Divine
Sacred
Important
Epic
Love yourself epically
I'm a Doctor of the soul
And here is my prescription for you
Do this everyday
And you will be whole

Is this America?
I saw Jesus today
He was sad
They made him cut his hair and Don a Wall Street suit
He said he didn't like his new job
Selling guns and hate
I said I get it
Your use to feeding the poor healing the sick
I said
This isn't your bag
Not that Jesus ever had a bag
He was homeless in fact
His bank account was empty
But his heart was full of God
And love and mercy and compassion

I don't like that Osteen guy he said
He sells me for cash
I said I don't like him either
He has teeth like a shark
And crocodile eyes
God is on fire right now
And his heart weeps at what he sees
Is this America dad?
My 14 year old daughter Sophia asks
Watching angry people in Buffalo skins
With flags
Storm the castle on tik tok
No sweetie it's not
I reply
America is greater than this

God's new commandment
Love everyone
And abhor hate
God is weeping at what he sees right now
His angels are comforting each other
They watch as his sons and daughters
Slaughter one another
You've chosen the golden calf again
It will lead you nowhere

But to hell
And destruction
And permanent loss
Do you even see the little ones watching?
They are mine you know
Love everyone
And abhor hate
Lay down your arms
And your schemes
And your hate
Paint love and not disgusting hate
Look at yourself
Do you really think you represent me?
Then you don't know who I am
Hear my words
Turn from this
Your hate
Your fake power
It will destroy you
And many with you
Don't follow the golden calf
Look for the fire I place in his eyes
Look for the fiery hands that heal
The host of heaven are his guides
Love everyone and abhor hate

He that hath an ear
Many climb tall buildings believing they can fly
And are wrong
They believe strongly
They have faith
Yet the mountain will not move
It crushes them
In their stupidity
The ultimate reality check
Is eternally embarrassing
The king doesn't want this
You do
There will be no turning back
You've read a book on how to fly a plane
But you are no pilot
And have never sat in a cockpit
Yet you tell others how to fly
You will only crash
Turn from hate
Abandon your anger
And what you think is power
God only talks to the least
The fool
The outcast
The nothing
You think he rides in a limo
Fool
Shelter the poor
Feed the hungry
Clothe the naked
He commands this

Tremor
Eating lunch alone again
Good morning texts have ceased
I knew they would I enjoy them while they last
I feel human for a bit
And not the horned hoofed beast I really am
I even wore deodorant for her
Didn't want to stink
In California the quakes are accepted
A given
I doubt people get used to it
And the long periods of quiet
Are a moment of respite and peace
And then boom out of nowhere startling quakes
Destruction
And gone
Silence again time to recover
Unfortunately love or the pursuit of love is very similar
Well at least it is for me
For you it may be easy
Or have worked out
And I say to you
Up yours
You're lucky
Lilith didn't like her position so she left Adam
Was Adam Hurt?

Did Adam Try?
At all to get her to stay
Was there even an attempt at give and take?
Was God a shitty marriage counselor?
So off Lilith went and became a beast
I'm a beast now of sorts
I've read of love in books
Seen it in movies
I don't like my position either
Of fool
So the dark wood is my home
We're all beasts here
All of us
We don't fit anywhere
And our love is wild
And strong
And unhinged
Come to me
Don't be afraid of my horns
Or wings
Or hooves
Nor my red skin
I will love you wildly
Our love will be a ghost
That will haunt heaven
Tell me what you want
I'll give it all to you and more
Come be a beast with me
And we can be free

The finger of God
Can we find you in all of this dirt and grime?
Are you looking for us?
Like a parent looks for their toddler who has wandered off in the store
Where are you?
Where are we?
Drowning in hate and violence
Are you gone?
Are we gone?
Too far
Will

Angels come and set us straight?
Is it too late for love?
Have we sold our souls for paper airplanes?
Will a prophet arise with fiery eyes and heart to show the way?
Can we hear your voice thru him?
Will he point the direction we should go?
To stop all of this madness and chaos
Children are watching
And they are so scared
Will he be the finger of God?

How to be a sad poet
Drinking helps
I'd suggest vodka

Oh and love someone deeply who doesn't love you
That will do the trick
Swim in that for awhile
Drown almost in it if you will and the only lifesaver will be putting
your abyss into
Sad
Sad
Words
Have big expectations
About
God
Love
Life
Sex
Money
Politics
And have those all go unfulfilled
When your plate is always empty
And every door you knock at slams shut in your face
And you've nowhere to live but the dark woods
And you're an outcast
And always getting 4th place
Then
With those feelings for ammunition
You'll load the gun of poetry
And fire away

The girl in the red wool coat part 2

I can't sleep
I've argued with you all day and you're not even here
There must be a doctor who can cut you out of my mind
Is that even the location
To be honest my hearts been involved for years
Why are you so mean ?
I just don't understand
How Cold you are
And ruthless with people's names
You are
I don't understand myself either
I've worshipped you since high school
So you're basically a god
And not the nice kind
I waited and I waited like that guy in the notebook
But you didn't want me as a disciple
I've seen who you choose to have religion with
And your standards are a bit beneath you
I'm not beneath you
You looked at me like I was
If I truly was beneath you you'd be a very happy goddess not to
brag just saying

Dark wood
I live in the dark wood
Because I am a beast
I tried to be an angel
But I wasn't very good at it
And my hooves gave it away
I tried to hide them under a coat
But she knew right away
As I gallop and don't fly
All the lonesome losers live here
In the dark wood
Belonging is for others
Acceptance not my gift
When you pass the dark woods
If you're an acceptable
It looks very frightening
But to me it is home

Trial
We all worship
There is no escaping it
Some people worship power
Some people worship money
Some people worship sex
Some people worship love or the idea of it
We all worship
We serve some God
God is our job
God is our marriage
God is our money
God
Is a verb
Singing does not impress him

Nor do book deals
The hymn that God demands to be sung is the act of love for the
stranger
The neighbor
Think of the person in your heart
That you hate
That you despise
That you judge
Think of them
This enemy who is beneath you
God requires
You lift them up
Lift them up
Above you
Cleanse your heavy heart of hate and anger
Become like your father
Whose sun shines on all
The scales are waiting
Will your heart be light as a feather?
Or fat with hate and eternal punishment
Love
I beg you

Entertaining angels
Would Jesus wear a leather jacket?
Would Christians think he was strange?
All of this talk about love
And the poor

And cheeks
Weird
I don't see you at the capitol
I don't see you in a suit
I see you at a food pantry
Multiplying the heads of lettuce so there's more
And turning Coke into water because that's a healthier choice
I see Jesus watching the news and weeping
I see Jesus holding the hands of someone dying
And just listening
Listening
Listening
Listening
There's allot of talking right now
And all of it is hate
And violence and chest puffing
And the road to hell

Give me rest
Wrap your wings around me
For my eyes are heavy
And the wound in my heart is deep
It's been pierced by one I thought was my brother
My friend
Give me rest
O lord
For my fire goes dim
Breathe into me
Your life giving breath that I may be renewed and rekindled
Hear me Abba
Hear me Abba
I've never needed you more than now
Give me your manna
Make my cup run over with your love
I'm drowning in all of this hate
And anger
I can't breathe here anymore
The oxygen is thick with sin without remorse
There's no shame now
It doesn't exist in a foolish heart
And there's fools everywhere
I'm knocking at your door
No guns
No roses
Let me in
Heaven can't be seen from here
The smog of hate is too thick
They want more people to die
More people to suffer
I just want rest
Rest in you

I Frankenstein
Many people mistakenly think that
In Mary Shelley's book the monster is called
Frankenstein
It is not
The monster is never given a name
Just life
And unquenched desires
And limitations and differences that make connecting impossible
But daily strangled by the desire to do so
Everyone's the monster in reality
We wrestle with our creator
Asking why
Why am I here
Why did you make me?
For what purpose
Why am I unfulfilled?
Do I truly have to wait on heaven for satisfaction?
Why
And don't get me started on questions of love
That's when things can get serious or dark
And unmet needs can make monsters of us all
And isolation
Let me tell you about isolation
And what that can do to you
Do you have time?
Maybe I'm wrong
Maybe the mad scientist who sheepishly gave life is the monster

And the monster is Frankenstein
Or that deep dark unfulfilled part of him he refused to let out
So he gave birth to his dark passenger
In the only way he knew how
And that's why now free of it the mad scientist rejected his child
And his child became an orphan
Forever chasing him
Forever chasing being human
Forever sad
But wait maybe this isn't about revived corpses
And lightning bolts after all
Maybe the book itself
Is the monster
And the author
Mary Shelley herself is the scientist
Scapegoating her feelings onto pages and a lifeless fiend
Feelings of an unfulfilled life and marriage
And a culture that did not accept female authors
Maybe
Just maybe
That is the real beast in flesh
Love would be nice
I just keep writing these poems
I can't stop
I guess God has something to say
If you ask me he never shuts up
Well lately
Always grabbing my pen
Putting it in my hand and saying
David say this
David say that
David be honest
Ugly is beautiful to God
He wants all our pain
All our heartache
We don't have to lie
We're broke
And broken
And ugly
Ugly is beautiful to God

Can't you feel it?
Close your eyes
Listen to your heart
This isn't home
He is
He is
He is
Waiting on us
To stop this
And come home

How to walk on water
Did you know a spider saved King David?
It's true
The Bible is full of miracles
Giants and slingshots
Seas parting
Burning bushes
Really nice lions
I mean really nice lions who don't eat you
When you're stuck with them

There's more just wait
People raised from the dead
Water to wine
I'm
A vodka guy myself
What is a miracle?
A miracle or an act of God is something out of the ordinary that doesn't
usually happen
And in these dark times that can be allot
Love for example it's not very popular
Be a miracle for someone today
Say hello to someone ask them their name
Treat people with dignity and kindness
Be a friend to your enemy
You know who I mean
Be a miracle in someone's life today
Listen
Listen
Listen
Everyone's talking but no one is listening
Listen to someone's heartache
Just listen
Don't offer advice
Just listen to them as God their father does when they pray
Find the sick
Put a basket of food on their porch
Look at someone with new eyes see the good in them
Tell them about it out loud
To be rich is to be poor
Give away your love
The world needs it now

Supervillain

Every god needs a devil
The first line of the poem
Is ridiculously heavy with meaning
We all think we're gods
Of course we're the hero of the story
But not everyone who crosses us is the devil
Read that again
We feel terrible about ourselves many times
So we step on the skulls
Of others toward a stronger self esteem
Nothing can make you feel better than trashing someone verbally
Did you hear?
Did you hear?
I can't prove it but I know
I know
They're bad
Bad I tell you
Me
Why silly I'm good and virtuous
And my number 2 smells like Chanel number 5
Do I own a mirror?
I do I hardly look at it
It'd be too painful
I'd have to face myself
My sins
My vices
My mistakes
No I'll just judge others
I'm not a judge you say
That's Gods job
He owns the scales
Then what else am I going to do to feel superior to someone
You tell me
I pride myself on my ability to judge
And murder with my thoughts and words
And everyone should know what I think
Right?

Patmos
In exile I sleep
Watching the world burn with hate and anger
Tanks roll down the streets
Of capitols
Angry men head to Washington with guns
Hate
Hate
Hate
Courses thru the veins of the country
The beast
Is being worshipped
He is arrogant in his speech
And crafts wickedness with his tongue
Nothing but death results
You worshipped an idol
You've lost your way
Does this look like Jesus to you?
Puffed chests
And power grabs
Power
Everybody wants to rule the world
Tears for fears
There will be lots of tears
Our children are watching
Our children are watching
Our children are watching

Possessed
I am possessed
God has overtaken my soul and set me ablaze
I am the least
An outcast
Scum of the earth to some
A loser to others
Why is God inside of me?
Why me
I do not know
But he has something to say
About now
Right now
I do not have a pulpit
I have no lineage or family tree
Yet I feel him possess me
And flow thru my soul like a brook
I am not a proper candidate to speak for him
I am a sinner
I cuss like a sailor
I drink vodka
I gamble
If you were to say you're no man of God
I would agree wholeheartedly
There is nothing righteous or holy about me
I started writing again to cure my broken heart over a woman
Then God showed up

Did you hear me?
God showed up
And said take this pen
I have something to say
My children are in trouble
Like Jonah I want to flee
But I watch the news
And I know
I know
The world needs Love
Now more than ever
I will submit
I will write
About loving everyone and abhorring hate
And loving your neighbor
Everyone's your neighbor
You see

The wages of sin

Once I worked a job doing almost nothing but with great pay

Once I worked a job that bloodied my knuckles and ached my heart and soul and was paid almost nothing

Your boss determines your pay

As well as your job

Who is your boss?

What is your job?

That is simple

God

Love

God the honest paycheck writer

Will weigh your deeds in the end

He will hold your heart in his right hand

If it's full of love and a life lived pursuing peace

Great is your reward

The wages of love are everlasting

If it's full of hate and a life of judging others

Being blind to the pain and suffering of others

Being indifferent to the poor

The lonely

The prisoner

The stricken

Terrible will be your soul's journey

God is tired of apologies

And excuses

Your actions carry eternal weight

And you will be weighed by them

Be careful

With your thoughts

With your deeds

You will carry them all with you

Before his throne

The lion doesn't sleep tonight
Find your rest in me
All you who are tired and weep
The world is not as it should be
But I am with you
Look to me
I will guide and keep you
Look to me
I will give you rest
Pray to me
Give me your heart
My water is cool and refreshing
Come to me I have new garments for you to wear
Of fine cotton
Cast off your old garments
They smell of the smoke of hatred and fear and fatigue
Cast those off
I love you so much
I know life has been hard
I know you hurt
You are so important to me
You are my daughter
You are my son
I am your father
I will never leave you
I will be with you always
You are in my hand
Come to me

God at the bar
I saw God sitting at the bar today
He seemed very sad
The first shall be last
And the last shall be first
Because the last are always last
And least and leper's and spit upon by the elites of society
I asked God what he was drinking
He said water
I offered to buy him a drink
He said it's cool I'll turn it into wine later
I have two daughters
I love them very much
And want the world for them both
I worry about them constantly
That's why I'm sitting at the bar too
I've made mistakes as a dad
And let my girls down
I try though
I don't want them to be like me
I want them to be happy
And whole
I imagine as I look at him
What God must be thinking?
He has allot of children
I just have two
Parenting is hard
And heavy with importance
Your actions echo thru your child's life
As they age and become parents too
One day
And face the unfairness of love and life
I saw God sitting at the bar today

Professional boyfriend for rent
Valentine's Day is coming up
Why be sad and lonely
I'm the best
Really
Just don't ask for references
Because I've made allot of mistakes
I didn't listen when I should've
I left when it got tough
I was all about me many times
Well honestly most times
Whatever she was into I didn't care
I am guilty
Guilty
Guilty
I've been obnoxious
I've made jokes I shouldn't of
I've hurt her
And her
Is any ex I've ever had?
I'm not blameless
I'm so guilty
I own it
Own it
Own it
If love gives me one more chance
One more
I swear to god I will try harder
I do
I will listen
I will stop thinking of myself so much
I will shut up

I will
And I'll listen
I'll ask you about your day
I'll do dishes
I'll clean off your car
I won't leave
I won't I've been so guilty
And lazy
But love is work
It is
A job honestly
A job
I'm here for the position
Just don't ask for references

Kissing stone
All of my life kissing stone
Talking to cold marble
That never talks back
Never loves back
Never cares back
Never touches back
Like the happy care taker
I hold an umbrella over you when it rains
And clean the leaves off of you in the fall
And brush the snow off of you in the winter
One day
You'll return the favor
One day you'll love me
One day you'll awake
I touch your marble
And you're cold
I wish you were awake
I've spent my entire life waiting
Waiting
For you
But you don't even move
You don't even breathe

You don't even care
But I'll just stay here taking care of you
One day
One day you'll wake up
I'm sure

Fake
Are these the shoes I should wear?
The coat I should wear
The clothes I should wear
To be acceptable
To be loved
To move with the flow of the crowd
Uninterrupted
I want to blend in
Don't want to stand out
It's lonely outside to pack
I've seen those who don't conform
They talk loud
And dress funny
And say there's another way

Another way
Should I talk like this?
Stand like that
Say I love you twice
Sit in that pew
Listen to that song
Drink that
Smoke that
Think that
Tell me what I have to do
To fit in
To belong
It's allot of work
But I'll try
I'll try
Being real
And choosing for myself
That's hard
I need told
Is everyone else doing it?
Cause I'll do it too
Don't want to be free
That's scary
People will point fingers at me
And talk
And judge
And I won't get the best seats at anything
People won't say hi
They'll be afraid of me
Of being me
Of the freedom I have
I'll just be fake

Zipporah
The rarest diamond in the world
Does not compare
To the beauty of a virtuous woman
Her hands feed the poor
Take care of the sick
Wipe the fever from her child's forehead

Her mind makes lists
Of things to do to make the lives of those she loves better
Her heart
Her heart
Her heart
Loves like a raging lion
Those she's granted refuge in it too
Her heart is a home
A sanctuary
That you may find peace in forever
Look in her eyes
See that fire
She's the daughter of God
No one is like her
God smiles at her daily
She resides in his heart
She is his agent
Her mouth prays for those
In need
In pain
In trial
Her voice
Her words are carried to the ears of God himself by legions of angels
Her children are counted blessed
Her husband runs home to her everyday
For she restores his weary soul
In the storm
She is the shelter
All sprint too
What ruby or diamond or emerald even compares
She's the daughter of God you know

Doctor Manhattan
Run away with me
I have a ticket to Mars
I'm going there
I don't want to be alone anymore
And earth is the loneliest place there is
We can't breathe up there you say
We can't breathe down here either
It's either dangerous or illegal
The air on earth is polluted with hate and thick with contempt
Go with me
I'll make us a castle
And whatever you want
We will just make it
Don't bring anything from earth
This place sucks and I don't want to remember it
But I do want you with me
If that's cool
Can it be cool?
I'm tired of being here
Same shit everyday
I'm drowning in the earth's sadness
I just want to be free
Free with you
Free from this
I'm tired of being sad and alone
And living in my mind
The rent there is expensive
Mars has pink sand you know
I just want to watch my toes dance in the sand
And feel the possibility of being someplace new
New
There's hope in that
I'm stuck and quietly dying and slipping into madness
Will anyone miss me when I'm not trying to save the day anymore?
People only seem to remember me when they're fucked and need my
help
That is so tiring
So

So
Tiring
Yeah I'm blue
Do you see any other blue people on earth?
I'm done being different
Different gets you exiled
Different gets your heart tore apart
Different gets you mistreated and beaten and burned
Holy shit
Nothing new happens on earth
It's all just a cycle with lulls in between of people taking a break from openly hating each other and killing each other to small quiet periods of just secretly doing so
Run away with me
To Mars
We can be the new Adam and Eve
And our politics and religion can be hand holding and love

Chasing devils
Are you bad for me?
Will you waste my time?
Treat me like shit
Gaslight me
Tell everyone I'm the devil who gave you the apple
If so
I'll run after you
With all my might
I'll chase you
Like a dog chases cars
I won't stop
I won't
Are you a sinking ship?
Call me rose and jack
Cause I'm aboard
Don't care what my friends say
Socrates can keep his advice
I just want you
To ruin me
And set me aflame in your wicked madness
I am the moth

I can't care about anything but you
I will be your love fool

Symptoms
I have a house full of shit
I've ordered but do not need
I spend hours and hours on Facebook
Watching people struggle to connect with each other
But stopping just short of really doing it
I'd sell my soul to hold her hand
What does skin feel like?
I have forgotten
I've gained 30 lbs.
During this pandemic
And it's all gut and ass

Sleep
Nap
Facebook
Coffee
More coffee
Try to work
I can't focus or think
And I'm afraid it's going to be like this forever
There's a new boss in the White House
Is he the same as the old boss?
Have we been fooled?
I am always fooled
I have great expectations for everything
First dates are always hopeful
Second date is always the reality check
As she invites me back to her place
And tries to put me in a big pot and cook me for her coven
I just want a better life
For me and my girls
Why does the card game of life always seem to have a stacked deck
when it deals me a hand?
I smile
And fold
Hoping for better
Next time
Next time

I had the best dream last night
I had the best dream last night

You were there for one
And God knows how much I love you
So you were there
And we were ok
Not like now
Not like the real world
So you were there
And I could tell you loved me
I just knew
I just knew
So you were there
You loved me
And you didn't want me to leave
Because I was at your parents' house
Your sister was there
So you were there
And I was walking out the door
Your parent's door
And you said
Come back in the morning we will have breakfast
And I knew from that
That I'd won
That you loved me
But then I woke up
So I don't know what we ate
Or if we ran off together
And raised cats
Like crazy people
Or fought at bed bath and beyond over comforter sets
That would make me happy too
Because
You were there

James Baldwin
The Apostle Paul said
The Love of Money
Is the root of all evil?
He was wrong
The love of yourself
Your skin
Your kind
Your kin
Your politics
Your God
And the hate of
Others
And by others
Those whose skin is different from yours
Those whose politics is different from yours
Those whose bank account looks different from yours
Those whose gender is different than yours
Those whose sexual preference is different than yours
Those whose address is different than yours
That
That my friend is the root of all that is evil
And the foundation of Satan's doctrine
In a nutshell
In a nutshell
To enslave people
And claim its Gods will
Is pure evil
Pure evil
God didn't need you to enslave anyone
For his truth to spread
For his love to spread

For his son to spread
And warm the faces of all of his children
Better listen to me
God writes this
Not me
Better change
Better repent
Hell is full of people who think they're good
And saved
And right
And true
But they were wrong

Yoga mat
I take my broken heart
To the yoga mat
My tired soul
That is beaten and bruised by life
My tense body
Full of anxiety and anger
And confusion
And I go thru my poses
One by one
And I breathe
I breathe
The breath of life
Back into my soul
And I stretch
And I breathe
And I stretch
And I breathe
And all of that bullshit
From assholes who hate
And throw rocks
On my path
I let it go

With every pose held
Every muscle tensed and relaxed
I slowly heal
Slowly let go
Because my body is a collector
A story teller so to speak
And when it gets full
Gets to be too much
My body begins to ache
Ache
Like my soul
For breath
For love
To be treated like a human
In a inhumane world

Take a picture it will last longer
I collect watches
It's an obsession
The ticking of the watch
Is a gentle reminder that the end of the movie is getting closer
When we ditch our popcorn and sodas
In the seat next to us and gently stretch and make our way to the streets
leading to the theatre
We just escaped reality in for a 2 hour movie
The light is blinding but we adjust
Having been so long in the dark
If you are lucky
And you will be
A few times in your life
You will touch moments

Created by the gods
Moments with your children
Moments with your soul mate
Moments when you win
And get to show your teeth and forget
About the cruel worlds bullshit
And the daily mountain climb
To drink from the cup of feeling human
That sits at the peak
Crawling with bloody knees thru thickets
Of your past regrets
And future mistakes
While wearing a 100 pound back pack
Filled with self-doubt
You only live once
I'm the angel of time so to speak
With a message
And that message is
Take lots of pictures
You're alive
And that's fucking beautiful
Take lots of pictures

Queen of hearts
Knocked on the doors of heaven
But when the doors were opened it turned out to be hell
There's a small stone in my shoe it's annoying
And I'm reminded by the situation of the imperfections of life

This all because of the fall I think
I think
Life would be perfect
If things were perfect
I miss you terribly
I'm so obsessed and crazy
And mental
And ugly on the inside
And maybe outside too
I miss my queen of hearts
All mean
And dressed in a red wool coat
With your scepter of judgement
I'm sorry I didn't impress
I bet
I bet
I bet
I could make you happy
And heal your heart
And fill it with my love
You'll be satisfied I swear
Please let me in
Forgive yourself for thinking I'm not the love of your life
I am

The truth about women
It's during the loneliest times that you understand what humans are made for
God was right
When he said man shouldn't be alone
He needs someone
To keep him on his toes
And ask him if he made his doctor appointment or not
Did you take out the trash?
Did you pick up the milk?
On the surface it sounds like nagging
But the angels know
The angels know this is what we need
Woman wasn't made from the rib of Adam
That's bullshit
And a huge step down from their proper place
You see Women are actually Angels who volunteer
That's the truth
God asks Angels if they'll come down to earth
And try to make this fucked up Eden better
And they show up
As tired moms
Exhausted nurses
Overwhelmed teachers
Hardworking doctors
Wives who never give up
Girlfriends who take us shopping and tell us that color does not suit us
Or it's time to exercise as our butts and guts are getting a little too big
And we need to shed some weight
Let's start walking together she says
What she really means is I don't want you to die human
I love being with you
I'd miss you if you were gone

Fall
Did Adam and Eve sleep allot?
When shit hit the fan
And the world wasn't as friendly anymore
How scary was the uncertainty
Of not knowing
Are we going to be ok?
Did Adam get tired of Eve buying shit from Amazon that they didn't
need
Couldn't God just chill out
It was just 1 apple
In reality a pomegranate
But I'll speak to the symbols you know
From Sunday school
Was the serpent an ass or a savior?
I don't know things are complicated
Sometimes our gods are devils and our devils gods
Today's savior is tomorrow's villain
What was the new normal like for them?
What was the old normal like?
Why was Eve so tempted so unhappy?
So unfulfilled
Adam didn't seem so happy himself
Is perfect not what it's cracked up to be
Is it boring?

Would we rebel against it?
Most likely
It happens every day
Someone walks away from the perfect person
Perfect life
Perfect family
Perfect job
Perfect gift
Perfect health
Perfect you name it
Insert your idea
I bet you
Yes you
Have walked away from your Eden
And years
Years later
You look back
And you try
You try so hard to lie to yourself and say
Yeah walking away was a good thing
The right thing
But in the dark corners of yourself lie
The hard truth
You know
You know
You left something good
You left someone good
You walked away
And you can never return

Goodwill hunting
I found my favorite book today at the Goodwill
Hemingway's
A moveable feast
The cover is almost sacred
And the pages are electric
With the tales of Paris

And cursing of death
I saw it hidden
Among those crappy 50 shades books
And knew I needed to rescue it
This book is a Faberge egg of literature
The priceless kind
It needed rescued
It's different
So am I
I need rescued
I hope you're reading this
My message in the bottle
I hope to go to Paris one day
I'd like to fence
And practice Savate
And drink coffee in cafes
And forget about who I use to be
Who people think I was or am
I'm tired of that
I turn the crisp pages
And it's like angels wings moving
To some angelic dance
That frees man's soul
I hope
I hope
I hope
You'll read this
And rescue me like I rescued this book
Tell me I'm different
And take me home
Your home
Then it will become our home
And every month will be august
With leaves falling
And days ending with us holding hands
Stalking thru our neighborhood
Our neighborhood
And our love can be
A moveable feast

Dunkin Donuts
I get it things are crazy right now
And who wants to be working
During this crazy time
And surviving
But we're here
I work all day on the frontline of mental health
And my teenage daughter eagerly
Eagerly waits for me to come home
And we head straight to you
It's our get out of jail free time
So to speak
We just want iced coffee
And a glazed donut
But the order is never right
And you guys don't even say hi or make eye contact when I pull up to
pay
And sometimes you just drop our order on the ground
And honestly
Honestly
This watered down iced coffee tastes more like water than coffee
And man that's allot of money for a shitty tasting coffee
And disconnected service
Can we change all of this?
Cause I'm not the only one
Coming to you with our offspring in tow
Not to lay something heavy in your lap
But this is our chance to taste being somewhat normal again and
escaping from all of this
And downing a good ole iced coffee and a donut of our choosing
That's all we want
Just that taste of Americana
Again
You are literally our souls smoke break
Could it kill you to say hi?
Maybe act like you want to serve us
Yours

The guy who makes annoying Facebook videos and poems
Dave

Like a book
Read me like a book
It's my path to heal
And let go and move on
And ask God questions
Hoping his angels will give me a message
I've been thinking about my cover
I want it to be basic and brutally honest
But the pages inside
I want them to be
Almost sacred
I say almost
Because
Nothing's been real sacred about my experiences lately
Nothing
I'm just frustrated with God
And life
And love
And anyone who breathes
I hope to sell lots of copies
When I'm done
I almost am
It's been a journey
I got my voice back
It's been awhile
I hope my book sits on your altar
Make my heart your religion
So to speak

I keep getting small stones in my shoes
It's annoying
Like love
Or hunger
Or thirst
Or coming to grips with the scary truth that you need all of those things
And it's very human
Very

Inside out
The kingdom of heaven is within
And so are the gates to hell
I search my self
Inside and I know I have issues
I want what's bad for me many many times
You ever do that
God talks to me in my dreams
And gives me the scoop
This is what you're doing that's holding you back
Your chasing death
Running to it
So to speak
Better to be alone and healthy
Than with someone and dying
I dig deep within my soul
With a holy flashlight
There it is
There's the issue that plagues me

And I face it
I face it
Because I'm wired
Weird
And love is hate
And close is far
And even when I'm with someone I'm alone
You ever feel like that
When Captain Kangaroo is your father
And Wonder Woman your mother
And shame and loneliness your steady diet
It can fuck you up inside as a kid
And as an adult
The Rabbi said the Kingdom of heaven is within
If I go there will I change the hell on the outside?
If I turn off the water in my soul
Will it stop raining in Kansas?
Let me click my heels together 3 times
Because I want to go home
I do
Nothing but cowards
Without brains
Or hearts here
And the wizards are fake
And the witches are real
Look at that monkey fly

Dear Nurses
I owe who I am today
To nurses who mentored me when I was young
And dumb
When I was young I didn't care about anyone
And I knew I needed to change so I worked at a nursing home
And you challenged me
You kicked my ass and set me straight

And put me on a proper path
To this day
I worship every one of you
And when you talk I listen
And when you say jump
I jump and then go get your favorite coffee and magazine
I watched you work doubles and triples
And summon Goddess like strength
I watched you hold the hands of the dying
And counsel the lonely
I watched in awe
At your feats of memory
And care
You walk a marathon a day
And stand up to Doctors who just don't get it
You don't need an invisible plane
Or gold bracelets
With your scrubs and stethoscope you quietly
Change the world everyday
Everyday
No parade or ribbons
Asked for
You just quietly sip your coffee and pass out love
Everyday
Everyday
In hospitals
And nursing homes
And doctors' offices
Royalty all of you
In the kingdom of my heart
Underpaid all of you
Saints all as well
I don't take the Vatican seriously because they never mention your feats
Are they stupid?
Or blind
You do miracles everyday
Then smile like it's nothing and wait for the next call light
Nurses

Mr. Darcy speaks

Words are weak
To convey the truth of something
Language is a virus
I want to fight you so bad
I hope I see you again
It will be epic
I promise
To challenge your thinking
I want you to tell me why I'm not good enough
I will return every serve like a tennis pro
John McEnroe who
You're taller than me
So I'll bring a stool
Words are weak to convey love
Truth
Or anything
They cost nothing
And fly out of the Mouth so freely
If I had to pay for words and their use
And the price was high
I'd be sparing in long sentences
And my words would be short
Brutal
And to the point
And heavy with meaning
Times 1000
So listen
Here what I say
It's not easy for men to do what I'm doing it's frowned upon
Considered weak
Your perception and opinion of me means everything
I'm always in court with you
Always
Am I guilty?
I am
Do I have a lawyer?
No
Did you know Satan was the first attorney?
It's true
My sin is you

I am in agony
This is hell
To love someone who abhors you
There I said it
Please don't make me say it again
The words cut my mouth and my heart
Like razor blades
Coming out
She only smokes when she cries
She only smokes when she cries
And no woman should ever cry
A broken angel with a stethoscope
Find comfort in my comforter
Escaping from hell never seems like heaven at first
Give it awhile
I check my phone for you all the time
What does that say?
I'm crazy
I'm sure
The only good thing about the world
Is the women who are here?
What if Nicholas Sparks doesn't really believe in love?
How ironic would that be?
Loneliness is my doppelgänger
I hope I spelled that right
I was baptized at Robert palmer's church
Smooth criminal
You have no idea
I'm going to steal your heart
Making deals at the crossroads
I'll play the violin for your soul to be mine
I'll even go to Georgia
Have you ever wanted something for so long you just can't turn back
now?
That bridge is on fire
Like my heart for you

Broken Bird
Birds with broken wings
Who cannot sing?
They use to
They use to
But something happened
Something bad
And they just wait
Wait to die
Wait for hope
Wait for something
Anything to happen
So that they can sing again
And fly again
And be birds again
Cause being broken
Is hell
And it's not their fault
That the thing that happened
Happened
And broke them

Broke their soul
Broke their being
Broke their life
Took their flight
And their song
Never
Never
Again
Will I let this happen to me?
Never
Never
Again
Will I be robbed of me?
Do you hear me?
Oh no you can't
Because I am a broken bird

I'd go to church with you
I'd go to church with you
I'd go to hell with you as well
Wherever you are
That's where I want to be
You're my religion
I am your biggest sinner
I'd love to be your saint
And drink coffee with you in the morning
I'd read your honey do list like a hymn
I swear
I'll never backslide

Or lose faith
Not in this
Not in you
Not in us
Not ever
I'll aspire to be
Who you want me to be
To gain access to your heaven
I don't need a big mansion
Just a queen size bed
With you in it
And two chairs sitting side by side
Facing the sun
So we can sit together
And side glance each other
Knowing we'd won
And the bullshit
Of fake lovers
Was gone
For good

Serpent in the garden
I've always been here waiting for you
I am low to the ground

And full of wisdom and thought
Not deed
I don't ascribe to that I don't need to
My landlord kicked me out long ago
Are you happy?
Are you content?
Are you ok
I'll convince you otherwise
Feel okay about your looks
Confident
I'll change that
I slither around the garden of your mind
The garden of your heart
And I lie
Lie
Lie
All day long
It's my craft
Don't feel good enough
That's me your welcome
Eat this apple
Don't turn it around though
It's rotten and full of worms
This devil needs no sympathy
I'm here to devour
On your left shoulder I sit
Hissing my poison into your heart
Into your ears
Ignore Michael on your right shoulder
He is no fun
And all in your corner
My character is set
If you could call it that
I see Gods sons and daughters
And I seek to devour them
Piss on their lives
Enslave them
To hate
To addiction
To destruction of the self

See that new marriage
I'll ruin it quick
Unity
Love
Empathy
Hold my hair back as I throw up
I'll have none of that
Peace
No thanks I'll take chaos
Any day
Be wise and run from me see my voice coming
I am easy to listen to
Easy to believe
Even though all I spew are lies
Michael
Is blunt
And holds Gods mirror to your heart
You should listen to him if you know what's good for you
But you won't

Medusa
Villain you say
Monster you suggest
Hideous you describe
I'm not the poet Shelley
Who fell in love with her too?
Long ago and defended her honor
I'm the poet Thomas
Who today
Many many years later
Loves her very much
I'll be her lawyer
Here is my case
Medusa
Was attacked and violated by Poseidon in Athena's temple
Instead of attacking Poseidon
Athena set her sights on Medusa
And Athena cursed Medusa an innocent
A victim
Cursed her in her stupidity
With vipers for hair
And a gaze that turns men to stone
Forever cursing her to live like a monster
Afraid and unable to love and connect
How lonely her life must be

Abuse victims know exactly what I mean
Abuse victims know the curse all too well
I hope my poem is better than Shelley's
You'll have to let me know
I think I understand her better
Love her deeper
I don't see what you see
No sword is necessary
She's not a monster
In no way shape or form
Look at her
Really look at her
Look at her eyes
You won't turn to stone
You may turn into a human
And learn to fight with love instead of hate

Confessions of an essential worker
I need a tattoo
And a beer
And a beach
With all of those beach noises blanketing my senses
I can close my eyes and feel the sand in my toes
And in my hands
I can taste the beer
It's a tall draft
I can see in my mind the tattoo parlor
The music is loud and heavy and most likely my favorite band
rammstein
You don't look like the kind of guy who gets tattoos they say
They always say that
I laugh
As I always do

And add to my spider tattoo collection
I'm so tired
But I can't be
Not now
Not for awhile
I dream of these things
Well my soul does
In my dreams all of this bullshit is over
No more masks
Or fighting
Or people dying
Or getting sick
Just me with my new tattoo
And my tall draft beer
Plotting out life lived on the beach
Maybe I'll sell shell necklaces
I wonder
Surely that will pay the bills
I want to totally forget about those as well
Bills
They don't matter here
I don't see any angels or burning bushes
Just seagulls speaking seagull and diving for their next meal
Oh one more thing
I'm a selfish guy to ask for more but
I'd love the juiciest cheeseburger there is
One that would make my doctor shit her pants
If she saw me eating it
The alarm sounds
My feet hurriedly hit the floor Dreamtime is over
I dress quickly but not fashionably
I haven't shaved all week
I look like a beggar
Time to pick up food and deliver it
And medicine as well
Maybe one day
One day
This dream will manifest
It's what keeps me going
The coffee in my cup

The gas in my tank
These are my confessions
I'm an essential worker

In my cage
In my cage I wait for you
Everything they say about me is true
I'm an animal
Not a man
Just a beast
I have no laws
And millions of flaws
Would you like to count them?
People without mirrors
Throw stones
Use me as your stepping stool
You never put me in family pictures
After you gave me your name
You text and text and beg to come back
Will no one else let you treat them vile?
I am in a cage so it's easy
She has the key
I think or hope
One of my personalities she will
 Like
Or love
And want to stay
They come on strong
In the beginning
Then slowly take off their masks
When they leave I'm super happy
Because it doesn't look like what the ad said
And there's no money back guarantee
And I lost the receipt
I want to be Bruce Springsteen
Only I can't sing I can write though I think
I'm a wandering beast like him
Never happy never content
Hungry heart
Yes I have one
These bars are cold

And I haven't ate for weeks
You have the key
If you'll be so kind
If you're a beast too
And I suspect you are
We could live in my cage
You and I
There's no need to be free
And passers by will come to our zoo and say
Look at those two
I wish I was like them
Together
See you in Paris
I'll wait for you
In the back of your mind
I'm Quasimodo the bell ringer
Victor Hugo would approve
You are my Esmerelda
I'll ring the bell for you daily and wait
Until your sentence is over
And you are free
Then you can come and dance for me
I'll listen to you sing
I'll forget for a moment as long as I'm with you that I'm the town
monster
And as we hold hands and take selfies in front of the Eiffel Tower
I'll be human again
You are my magic talisman
My form transforms in your presence
Bewitched by your grace
Of your love
You are the Gospel in the flesh
The spoken word
A messenger of God's love
And you have saved this hideous wretch
There's a difference between reading how to fly a plane and being able
to quote a book on flight page by page and actually being a pilot
Jesus would not recognize those who use his namesake as his today
He would be shocked
At the lack of love

His core teaching
Are you sure you're mine he'd say
And Christians would not embrace him
As well
I may go home in peace now the hand of God has touched me
And my tour of this
All of this is done
I'll be waiting for you in Paris
Always waiting for you in Paris

Photograph

I sleep with your photograph by my bed

It is worn and stained with tears

And slightly crumpled as I cling to it at night

Today was shit

So I pull out my photograph of you

It's my Bible

So to speak

I take you everywhere I go

I know every line and contour of your face like a great monument

That exists in my heart

You're sitting at your kitchen table

And you're looking at me not smiling like I need to do the dishes and you've asked twice

I love that face

I love you

And have since we were young

And I know your secret

You love me to

I tried talking you out of your marriage

For selfish reasons actually I'm no saint

That was long ago and you didn't listen

So look at us now

I stare at your cross necklace that adorns your amazing neck and I'm pissed I didn't buy it for you

And all of this time has passed and he's not me

Your faith is beautiful you love God so much

I'd build you the biggest church I could

With all the gothic trimmings you like

I'll be your gargoyle

True Daughters of God are hard to find

I'd repent for you

Yes I would

In the pew every Sunday with you next to me

Eyes

Sometimes brown

Sometimes green

With a Queens crown of Salt and pepper hair

And a heavy heart that's felt so much pain

And carried the weight of others

I am a dark winged thing

Possibly the devil himself

That's me

I'll be honest

You are the water in my flask

When I've been stuck in the desert for days

You are gone now

I can feel it

But I hold your picture in both hands

Staring into it like an abyss

For it is all I have now

That you are gone

Askew
When you see the world in black and white

Good and evil
And no In between
When you can mark people good or bad
And bang your gavel
And place them in a cell
Of your choosing
When on your throne you know who people should be
And damn them if they don't
And even if they do
Cause its fun to be better than everyone
Isn't it
Feels good
Don't have to drink the poison of my fallacies
Or past mistakes
I bought my crown
I get to use it
My gavel is my own
Bang bang you're bad
I'm good
There it is
I walk sideways and at an angle
My ground is shaky
I cross my eyes to see straight
Everything is askew

Wait

On you

I wait

I'd step out of line but my heart was here first

The heart what a strange thing it is

Does it know something I don't?

About you

About love

About us

You live in my head

And in my heart

Men are scared of this kind of talk

Men are scared of feeling this way

I am not

I'll tell you to your face

Every inch of you is sacred to me

I think you're a witch

Because I just can't shake you

Or let you go

You are inside of me like breath

I bet Shakespeare loved someone

Like I love you

I bet his Facebook page was full of crazy lovesick poems

About some woman he couldn't forget

Or maybe even have

And people rolled their eyes

And thought he was a loon

100 years from now people will read my book

And go wow what's it like to love someone like that

Or be loved like that

And did he eventually win

These crazy poems were written during a pandemic

When people were dying

How can anyone think of love?

To them I say

Hell makes me think of heaven all the time

And boy you should see her

You should see her

Fake ass friends
Judas betrayed Christ with a kiss
We just smile and pretend we're cool with people nowadays
Who we are secretly pouring gasoline on and setting on fire
And when we're caught
Or our venom is discovered
We say who me
I'd never
Betray you
Sell you out
Talk shit about you
Leave you in the dust
Or hanging
Judas hung himself after
Did you know that?
Tried to give the money back
Realized his sin

His best friend was God and he fucked him over sold him out
Can you imagine?
That
I bet you can
It's the harshest truth to love someone and have them betray you sell
you out
It's like a butcher cutting off your hand
The phantom pain
Of the missing limb
Lingers
And reminds you that you're somehow missing a part of yourself
You lost your friend

Strait jacket
Tied up in my mind
Been starving so long
I overeat at the thought this could be love
I'm so stupid

I always am
The way I hope and long and desire
I'm so stupid
My hands aren't tied
And neither is my heart
There's always this thick ass glass between me and what I want
What I love
I bang and scratch and plead but that glass is thick
And my knuckles bloody from trying
I gasp for air but cry acid tears
I'm too much for what I want
Too much for my desires
My reality
I should be in a strait jacket
The world don't want me free

Sleeping pill
I can't sleep
Dreaming is forbidden here it seems
Nightmares only
The wind is cold with winter
My bed is empty and freezing
The heat must be off
I lay here patiently like a death row inmate
Awaiting my sentence
What will happen today?
What will happen tomorrow?
If I could dream
Room on my bed would be sparse
Your eyes would be my alarm clock
I've been alone all of my life
Even when I wasn't
I'd finally clean off my old kitchen table so we could eat breakfast
We break the rules and sit side by side sharing ear pods so we can listen
to 90's music before our real life begins
Our fake life is much more nice
I can sleep now and so can you
We dress quickly and tag team making our bed and then rush to the
kitchen and tag team the dishes
Don't want to have to deal with them when we return from our real life
You wash I dry and put away
We kiss each other in a Disney way
And then we jump in our cars waving goodbye at each other
I do not want to put it into drive
This is all I have ever wanted or lived for
I'll see you again at 5
And then I can be human again

Thoughts and prayers
Off your knees time to fight
And get dirty and bloody
And encumbered by life
Your brothers and sisters are in trouble
The only angels who get respect in heaven have dirty wings
And bloody knuckles
And black eyes
And scars for medals
God is praying to you
To act
In this dark time
Get up and love someone
Fight for someone
You know what to do
Love
With a capital L
Like all life depends on it and it does
Don't seek your own comfort
Seek the comfort of others
Don't seek your own joy
Seek the joy of others
Look at that hobo walking the street
Holding a street sign
He's your brother
Look at that girl stealing from Walmart
Cause she can't feed her babies

She is your sister
Stones
Throw those down
You have better things to do with your time
With your life
The world is waiting for you
God is waiting for you
The question is prayer
And you
You are the answer

The world's sexiest poem
Shapes in the dark
Can barely make them out
One of them is me the other is you
Not knowing where one ends or one begins
We love in the dark
We escape from the light
It's cold there
The dark provides electric heat for our love
With neon counseling
Candles are sexy but not necessary
As we are both aflame with love
Two long waiting embers who finally connected
And set this cheap twin bed and quilt on fire
Ashes everywhere by morning
We will need a new place to stay
We escape this pyre of a mansion with nothing but the love on our
backs
That is all we need

Two demons who have rebelled and created their own religion
Each being each other's altar

Vows
Words
Magicians use words to secretly shape the world
Words are powerful
Monks in a cave in Tibet
Chant words that bring enlightenment and peace to a whole country
Words
Authors create whole worlds with just words

And you buy it
And read it
And live in another land in your mind's eye
Words shape things alter trajectories give things power
Words
Two people everyday
Stand across from each other
In front of God and his representative
And use words to declare their path
You are who I want
I want to grow old with you
Words
I want you till I die
Words
If things go south I'll stay with you
Words
I think of you everyday
Words
I love you
More words
I'll wait for you
Words

Piñata
I am done with all of this
I am done with all of you
Was the birthday party fun
I didn't get an invitation
It's a small town
Slander travels fast
People don't have anything better to do
Decades of being there
Saving the day when needed only to realize you're just a punching bag
For peoples low self esteems
Your mirrors are all broken
And your words cut like expelled kidney stones
You only need me to make yourself feel good
But in reality you're a wretch
Who hasn't taken your very own existence seriously
You can't hit what's not there
So that is my new game plan
You strike and strike and poke and ignore and make fun of till the
candy flows
That is over
You'll need to hit yourself
But that would hurt you say
There now
That's the spirit

I'm not good
I'm not good at this
Whatever this is or maybe
And generally I tend to make a mess out of everything
By thinking the wrong thing
Or saying the wrong thing or getting the wrong idea
About
Well everything
So if you have it in your head
That Prince Charming will ride up
And sweep you off of your feet
And you will be in awe every 5 seconds of me
It's probably not me you're looking for
In fact I can almost guarantee you
I'm a square peg
In thought
In language
In deed
Whoever she is
That I'm supposed to grow old with
She will have to be very wise and special
I'm a wild animal
I've not been tamed
Oh I'm broken alright
But not like a horse
I'll never be broken like a horse
If you come in my cage
Nervous
Or with wild demands

Or anything but love
I will snarl and growl
And shake my bars till you leave
I am a beast
I make no apologies
I don't want to waste your time
There's no gold in this heart
Only passionate darkness
If you give me peace
And see more than a beast
And show me your heart thru your eyes that truly see me
I'll love you like no man ever could

More please
I'd like more
As I hold up my bowl
That is empty of course at the table of life
And I ask very politely like Oliver Twist
Please sir may I have some more
More of what you may ask
More love
More friends
More happiness
More wine
More of everything please
Less worry
Less stress
Less loneliness
Less pain
That would be great

Another day without you
You're gone and not coming back
Your picture rests on the chair by my bed
You're a ghost now
Haunting not my house but my heart
I talk to you sometimes
Your picture that is
You do not answer
If you did I'd be in trouble
The loneliness I feel is thick like a wall meant to keep people out
I wonder what if allot

In my mind's eye I vacation from all of this
And you are there with me
You help me try on clothes and pick out shirts
We eat together and talk about our days
We sing at church using only 1 hymnal we don't need two
We do dishes together and talk as we do it
We're always talking
That's what I like
The silence is gone
It has retreated
I wait for you here in my dark lonely room on my cheap twin bed like a
death row inmate waits for his last meal
Last rites
A stay of execution is not possible
I think
Because you're not coming back

Pillow
I just want you

On the pillow next to me
I'm the devil
Who will give you whatever you want
Life without you is hell
And cold and lonely
I stare out into nothing
And see your face in the cups of my hands as I start to dive into them to weep
That I'm almost 50
And still don't have you yet
Aches my heart to bits
I cleaned the bathroom today and washed the bedding
I always leave room for your tooth brush and combs
And space in my closet
Hoping you come home

In the beginning
Adam and Eve were together but not really together
Arranged marriages are a scary thing
I bet Adam wasn't a talker
And the snake was
Things weren't perfect after all
Or the longing wouldn't be been there
It's the longing
That truly changes things
The unmet needs
That are doorways
To apples
God was playing God
And it failed big time
Even with divine backing things can go south
Maybe that's the lesson
I'm sure there were moments
Moments when it was working
And Eve was happy
And Adam was happy
And they looked like a couple
But things happen
We get those moments in life
Moments of perfection
When everything is okay and right with the world
Better savor those
Maybe Eden
And here's the big lesson
Isn't a forever thing
Maybe Eden is just moments
And that's why God invented cameras

My favorite Ghost
You're gone now
It seems
I was walking at the mall today
And stopped by the tuxedo shop display
Do you think they'll make it?
I wondered
Those two headless mannequins
Love does that to you,
 You know
You lose your head
And your heart
You get all dressed up
What's the special occasion?
Starts with a date
Then that date turns into another date
Then that date turns into love
And the next thing you know
There's two of you
God's sacred math
And you want to be together
Forever it seems
There you two are standing headless

And in love

Spring
It's February 7th
The sun is shining thru my blinds
Kissing my skin like a reunited lover
Who strayed for whatever reason?
But has seen the error of her ways
And has returned with a vengeance
Making war with the cold that rules and haunts the season
I knew it would show
Eventually
March 20th is the official day
Spring is looked so forward to because of the harshness of winter
A welcome reprieve

A cold glass of water
After a hard ran marathon
Glimmers of hope will appear
Days when the sun shows up and says who is boss
Or that I'm coming
The sun
The great lover of us all
In Dante's inferno hell is not hot
It is cold like Ohio
No wonder the devil never visits here
I await you dear spring
I look forward to planting myself on a park bench and watching ducks
swim by
Couples with strollers
And great expectations
Walk by
Squirrels arguing over territory
Sing a song only nature understands
The dance of seasons and we are its partner
So to speak

I love you like a Michael Bolton song
Oh how I love you
Let me not count the ways but give the perfect metaphor

I love you like a Michael Bolton song
That 90's prophet of love
If I said I didn't love you I'd be lying
If I said I don't think about you all the time
And that you're not always in my thoughts I'd be lying as well
Steel bars
Uggh
They seem to keep us apart
I'm not supposed to live without you
Ever I think
Because your soul provides me with the nourishment my lonely heart
craves
Time way too much of that isolated and without you
Love I have a Fort Knox vault of it waiting for you when you're free
Tenderness I swear to not be an ass like other men or not as frequently I
promise
Is love a wonderful thing
It sure can be if you're with someone who is a team thinker who know
loves a dance of give and take and when your partner is in the ring you
better be in her corner with the spit bucket
When you're back on your feet again
I'll be there to swiftly sweep you off of them
And show you something new
A love so beautiful
We can top that I think
Darcy and Elizabeth won't compare
That's what love is all about trying to do better be better so to speak
Can I touch you there pointing 1 index finger at your heart?
And 1 at your mind
Cause that's where I hope to stay
Everyday
Every minute
Every year
Happy Valentine's Day

Depression
Well I'm sad again
Some days I'm ok
Some days I'm strong
Some days I'm weak
And dark
And can barely move
And I feel hopeless
And a waste of human flesh
I get stuck in this quicksand
Like an old 80's action show character
When I was a kid I thought quicksand was everywhere
And it is
But it's between your ears
I'm not playing possum
I honestly can barely move sometimes
And the fire has been blown right out of me
My fists unclench
And my fighter's stance drops into a fetal position that I have to crawl
my way out of
My mind plays a horror show of past mistakes
And future predictions of darker times
A loveless death
A loveless life
I jump on an ember of flame somewhere in my heart hiding
I summon it
For strength
For courage
For guidance
As I escape from the coffin that is my bed
I lace up my running shoes

And put on my Nike shorts
My altar is the Keurig
That is making me a cup of inspiration before my feet hit the road
Men aren't allowed to be weak
Or sad
Or lonely
Or to lack confidence in the future
Or to be knocked down by life in the 5th round
But we are
Human
So I rise
I rise and I run
To beat this
Depression

Divine bucket
On the subway I sit and people watch
But I see more than people
At the airport I sit and listen and watch
I see more than Ants coming and going on the fast track of life
Sitting in my uncomfortable seat on the bus
I see an elderly woman
Sitting across from me I see vast history and time
And lovers and husbands and competitions lost and won and children
raised and jobs worked all concealed in a suitcase of wrinkled skin
And graying hair
What are we I think deeply?
Surely we're not these suits of skin and flesh
That break down and grow old and die
Surely we are more than time passers
On the time clock of life
A poet brings forth words to the page
They are emanations of the poet a part of the poet and in essence the
poet himself
We are Gods Poetry

His words made flesh
Drops from the divine bucket
Pieces of God wrapped in flesh
A divine drop from the bucket
Mixed in a wrestling match of anxiety and self-doubt
Struck the hardness of life and the work we experience
For we are not of this world
We are of God

Into the dark
Into the dark I go
Like someone driving into a storm
And getting out
Love is not real I've accepted that
Now
I am a fool
I've accepted that too
My beliefs were childish
And I'm ashamed
Back to being cold and primal I go
My pale white skin

Has grown coarse
And hard like a crocodiles
My heart has stopped beating
And returned to ice
My green eyes have turned black
My blood has slowed and gone frigid
I must do this you know
Change
Evolve
Let go
I can't survive believing
Believing
In love
Or happiness
Or hope
I live in the real world
I must adapt
I must evolve
The real world doesn't support those sort of things
Just look at it

I'll see you in my dreams
I like looking at you

I'd like to do it
Till we're old and gray
And our vision isn't the best
And we can barely hear each other
But we've got now
Now to memorize each other's voices
And facial expressions
And favorite foods
Likes dislikes
What your hand feels like in mine
I'll make you breakfast
And wait
I pause
Your face seems so at peace
And I know how hard you work
And you're not exactly a morning person
So I pause
Cause I'm taking note
It took forever to get here
So I drink this moment in
I pause
You own my favorite face
So I pause
And look at you
Really look at you
Cause I won
I'm so use to losing
But I won
Cause you're here now
Sleeping in our bed
Our
Can you believe I said that?
I sure can't
I write letters to you when I'm awake
I read them to you when I'm asleep
I'll see you in my dreams

Woman with a past
She has books on a tiny bookshelf by her bed
And a candle wrapped in a rosary from a long ago time when she had faith
An ashtray sits on top with ashes left over and Uncleaned from when she use to smoke and believe in God she has taken a break from both
She doesn't hold eye contact with people
She doesn't know her worth
She still swipes left and right
Even though nothing seems to work
She has brief moments during the day when she remembers the dance class she was in as a little girl
She misses that little girl
Parents divorced
And forgot all about her
Wrapped up safely in their own shields of hate and resentment for a love that made huge promises but failed
Her 9 to 5 barely pays bills
And her bed doesn't sit on a frame
But on a wooden floor speckled by paint scrapes
And pieces of past carpet
Her refrigerator is empty save a bottle of life water
And a can of tuna she knows doesn't need to be refrigerated
But keeps in there anyway out of habit
Roommates come and go and usually find love and leave to greener pastures
Her nails need done
But she can't afford that right now so she hides her hands
And leads with a quick smile
Cloaked in a cardigan that rescued her at the goodwill
There's a cigarette stain on the left sleeve but that's ok
It keeps her warm

And in lieu of pajamas sometimes
It is her bed mate

I miss you text
Choose your prisons wisely
100 cups of coffee and I still can't forget you
You texted me last night that you miss me
It was the highlight of my day
My words are weak
To convey how much you mean to me
Or what part of my lungs or heart I'd sacrifice
To hear your voice
I don't want to social distance with you
If you know what I mean
I don't want to wear a mask
Or be afraid of dying
You're a walking Bible
And I love that
I'm a walking sinner who desperately needs you in my life
I may be mad from isolation
But my heart feels you
And I haven't felt anything for years
Below my ears
I may not be good enough for you
I swear I'll try

God didn't talk to Moses all the time
It was bits and pieces
Those bits and pieces
Set people free
Created a nation
I hope you'll set me free
With fire
And part the seas of sadness that seek to crush me
Pharaoh won't let me go
I want a new life
A life with you
And 1 hymnal
And lots of talking
And tons of listening
My heart is a library of feelings for you

Alone
It's better to be alone
Than seek the ears of a fake friend
Who secretly strangles your character with their words behind your
back
It's better to sleep alone
Than to share your bed
With someone who shares a bed with everyone else
I'm all about sharing
But romantic love shared isn't very romantic at all
Better to be alone
Than with a taker

Who never gives or reciprocates
Or says thank you
Better to be alone than with someone who loves drama and causing chaos
Stand back and watch them
You would never have any peace with them
And your life would be miserable and exhausting
Life is forever high school with them
Everyone hates themselves
And uses the sins of others like anesthetic
To numb the pain of their self-hatred
And feel better by slander
If only for a moment
It's quite easy to do
Gossip and slander
And makes the ego feel elated for moments at a time
But the false healing fades and we must find a new victim to judge
Better to be alone

Welcome to Alliance
Cliques
Poverty
Racism
Unspoken of class war
Drugs
Bed bugs
Pastors who hate each other and call themselves
Christians
Small handful of the wealthy controlling everything
Don't you dare try anything here if you're different
From the caste
You won't succeed they won't let you
The old guard is still here
But not for much longer
Don't become hopeful
Their offspring have been trained to think like they do
They are ready to be your leaders
Your mayor
Your city council
Your city administrators
Nothing will change here
Nothing
A big college
A big hospital
And tons of poverty and lack
Children without beds
Parents blinded by meth
Do you have a recognized name?
Do you have money?
Are you even on the list?
If not sorry for your luck
Or lot in this life in this small city
Egos galore
Even though outsiders see it as a dying ghost town
No ghost would want to haunt
He who has the gold makes the rules
They say
And they're right

They do make the rules and keep things tidy for their country club
friends
And drain the citizens of tax money to support their habit
Welcome to alliance

My youth
I wasted my youth
In a bad marriage
Donated all those years in fact
That period in a man's life
When he has hair
And confidence
And strength like a bull
I gave it all away
To fake love
And now I'm old
And grey
And can't touch my toes
If there's a genie
I'd like to get that back
Be careful
In your youth
Who you give it too
That period of time when energy is infinite
And dreams abundant
It will be all be gone one day
And your years as a passionate lover
Will turn to years of being the wise teacher
Living in the woods waiting for seekers to learn from your mistakes

Haven't talked to you
Haven't talked to you in days
I think about you all day long
Your salt and pepper hair
Gets me thru my day
I just want to hear you talk
Even if you're mad
Or sad
Or glad
Your voice is my favorite song
I know it by heart
It's been 25 years
We've been doing this
Carrying you around like my favorite
Thing
It's the deafening silence
When your heartbeat is missed
And missing
That I can't forget you I try
God is doing something
Cause this spider always lives alone in his web

But hopes you'll get caught in it and stay
Stay awhile don't go
You live in my head constantly
And my heart
Can your stethoscope hear my vitals?
They are weak without you
I promise to be good
Just kidding
But not
I'll go by your definition
Of good and right and true
Basically I just want to make you happy
Whatever happiness is
Looked how whipped I am already
I am your dog
Sitting on the porch waiting for you to come home

East of Eden
God made man
Knew it wasn't good for him to dine alone
So he caused a deep sleep and created woman from his rib
1 commandment to follow
Just bear with me
Now there's a million
Started with 1
Became 10
Went up from there
Man is very creative
Just 1 commandment

Do not eat from the tree of good and evil
1 commandment
The tree was not evil
God can't create evil
Tree was good
1st ever sin was disobedience to a commandment
From God
That was the first sin
Serpent comes
Says nope things won't change you won't die
What died?
God's relationship with man completely altered
Man's relationship and woman's relationship with each other
completely altered
Both mans and woman's relationship to nature
For ever askew
Things die because of betrayal
Was God going to eventually let them eat from the tree?
You bet
We're they ready
Nope
Eating from the tree before they were ready is like trusting a 5 year old
with a chainsaw
Not ready
Chainsaw is not a bad thing but can cause great harm if someone
doesn't know what they are doing
Moral of the story
Don't jump into things you aren't ready for
Even if your slick friends tell you nothing bad can happen

Be my peace of mind
Can you be my peace of mind?
Can I call you my home?
Can I be honest with you about my sins my faults my mistakes
Can I be real with you?
Will you stay?
And not leave
And not entertain 10 guys in your inbox
And set up your next relationship while we're together like a chess
player
Plotting moves
Can I just lose my shit and cry with you
Cause I'm so tired
And men aren't allowed
To be human
Can I drink with you?
Think with you
Pray with you
Will you hold my hand?
Tell me the truth no matter how ugly that truth is
When I stand up in a crowd and say you're my girl
Will I look stupid?
Or a fool
I've been there
Did that
Done that
All before
Can you be different?
Can this be different?
Can you be my peace of mind?

Shuttered
Shuttered windows on businesses
Once hopeful American business owners
Now closing shop
Losing everything
Fighting to survive
The American dream has a virus
And everything is on sale
Job after job
Falling like a domino
Can't pay rent
And these food stamps are embarrassing
My old doctor doesn't take Medicaid
And the ones who do don't make eye contact
And hate treating you
And want you out the door quick
Mom and dad are fighting
They always are both want power and title
We just want jobs and to feed our kids
Politicians make promises
Like a teenage lover in the back seat of a dashboard lit car
Don't expect love
Or to be called back after the two backed beast is made
Or help
Or programs
That will save our businesses
Our families
Our health
Our way of life
They are comfortable and safe and well fed

And living large
With fat plates of food
And the best mistresses and clothing money can buy
The politician sits in front of the camera wearing a mask that he never truly wears
He pauses and removes it and uses that voice
The voice of the father or mother that we never had
I care they convey
From the comfort of their throne
Do they

Loud goats
In my cell I wait
I draw your face every day from memory
And write poetry to pass the time that you're gone
Minutes seconds hours
All run together
Has the isolation made me mad or honest?
About my prison sentence
And we all are in some kind of jail
Tastes of hell
When you're alone
And can't be with the person you love
I love you so much
I wonder if you know
Or care
Or understand
Or think I'm mad
I am you know
A highly functioning sociopath
I'll admit it
Broken to the core

Dark heart
Lightless except for the ember inside of me that loves you and my
daughters
Can you prove me wrong?
Invite the monster under your bed
Into it
I don't bite
Without invite
If you've ever wanted to own something dangerous
You do
And that's my love
I am a wild dog
Your wild dog
Happy Valentine's Day
Loud goats
In my cell I wait
I draw your face every day from memory
And write poetry to pass the time that you're gone
Minutes seconds hours
All run together
Has the isolation made me mad or honest?
About my prison sentence
And we all are in some kind of jail
Tastes of hell
When you're alone
And can't be with the person you love
I love you so much
I wonder if you know
Or care
Or understand
Or think I'm mad
I am you know
A highly functioning sociopath
I'll admit it
Broken to the core
Dark heart
Lightless except for the ember inside of me that loves you and my
daughters
Can you prove me wrong?
Invite the monster under your bed

Into it
I don't bite
Without invite
If you've ever wanted to own something dangerous
You do
And that's my love
I am a wild dog
Your wild dog
Happy Valentine's Day

We live in a society

Clears throat
Pauses
Scratches forehead
Where people like love laugh gasp dislike pictures of people
But never really ever connect to those people
For real
For real
And call that
A type of relationship
Friending?
Kind of strange
We live in a society
Where people worship politicians who don't give a rat's ass about them
They go to jail for them
They die for them
And these politicians don't even know your name
They don't attend your funeral
They don't testify for you in court
We live in a society
Where children are raising parents
And parents are getting high on whatever
They can while their kids become orphans and parents simultaneously
We live in a society
Where like a doll
Jesus is dressed into the image and likeness we want
And of course he's on your side
And not the side of the poor the down trodden the outcast the stranger
We live in a society
Where racism is legal
And it is illegal to have skin any color but white
We live in a society
Where politicians are rich
And children are poor
We live in a society
Where the wealthy prey on the poor
And use them to make their merch
Or for a photo opp pretending to be a good savior for social media
We live in a society
Where criminals enforce the laws
Where criminals make the laws

We live in a society
Where human life has no value
But for just $20.00 a month you can buy my fake bullshit that will do
nothing to your life but drain your pockets
We live in a society
Scratches forehead

Sex
You are completely predictable
And should be ashamed of yourself for just reading a poem with a
salacious title
This poem has absolutely nothing to do with said title so you can just
stop reading now and repent
Long pause
Long pause
Crickets chirping
Ok long pause over the worst people have stopped reading this
salacious poem with the provocative title and now I can be lyrical
because this poem is actually about said title
And people will gasp and be shocked
I may even lose my job
And the next job after that
Here it is
I look forward to the day we have a female President
It will say allot for our times

It may not happen in my lifetime but I hope it happens in my daughter's
lifetimes
I want them to believe
That all doors are open to them and possible
Regardless of their sex

Type cast
I'd like to be in a Nicholas sparks movie
Not as the funny side kick
Which is what I usually am
But well you know as the guy

I'm usually in a Stephen King movie though
I'd like to change that
In the beginning I think I'm in a Nicholas sparks movie
But then a priest appears and her head does a 360 and there's green pea
soup everywhere
And I go nope this isn't Nicholas sparks
Material
Sometimes I'm in a dean koontz movie
Well right now I am
It's a mix of koontz and king
There's disease famine and everyone's losing their shit
It's close to world war z
There's mindless zombies
But I don't have brad pitts cool
Scarf
I need a better agent
Because my movie parts suck
I was hoping to land a comedy this year
I'd be great in a bill Murray film
My career could use refurbished
I'd love to be in a Tarantino movie
Which maybe this is
The rock is in everything
Why is that?
Its 3 am I'm wide awake and bitching about my bit part
I kind of want to be the lead
No more being an extra for me
What movie are you in?

The man who fell to earth
I'm not from here
How does earth work
How do I blend in?
Pretend to be human
Chase money
And sex you say
Ok but why is that so valuable
Hate those who are different from me
Different religion
Different God
Different Skin color
Ok so to be human is to hate those that are different and chase money and sex
What else
Never be happy in the moment you always
Always need and want more and never ever feel good enough
Human enough or content
What about love that seems like 1 good thing you have on this planet?
Oh it is you say
But it's only reserved for those you don't hate
For those like you
For anyone who helps you get what you want
You're an animal who is never fulfilled
So to speak
What if I just love everyone?
That would not be normal
You would stand out
And be talked about
Ridiculed
Crucified
Crucified
Yes Jewish fella
Said the same weird shit 2000
Years ago
They killed him
Killed him

Take a picture it will last longer

I collect watches

It's an obsession

The ticking of the watch

Is a gentle reminder that the end of the movie is getting closer

When we ditch our popcorn and sodas

In the seat next to us and gently stretch and make our way to the streets leading to the theatre

We just escaped reality in for a 2 hour movie

The light is blinding but we adjust

Having been so long in the dark

If you are lucky

And you will be

A few times in your life

You will touch moments

Created by the gods

Moments with your children

Moments with your soul mate

Moments when you win

And get to show your teeth and forget

About the cruel worlds bullshit

And the daily mountain climb

To drink from the cup of feeling human

That sits at the peak

Crawling with bloody knees thru thickets

Of your past regrets

And future mistakes

While wearing a 100 pound back pack

Filled with self-doubt

You only live once

I'm the angel of time so to speak

With a message

And that message is

Take lots of pictures

You're alive

And that's fucking beautiful

Take lots of pictures

The boy with the spider tattoos
It's not your fault
It's not your fault
It's not your fault
I know why you care so much about the poor
I know why injustice pisses you off to the core
I know why you try so hard to change things
I know the thought of kids not having food or clothes kills you
I'm so sorry you were never a kid
And grew up alone
Living wherever you could
Eating out of trash cans
Fighting to survive
You were just a little boy
You were 11

It's not your fault
It's not your fault
It's not your fault
You wonder if deep down you are bad
You are not
The world can be a dark place
You can't fix everything
You only live once
I understand you
You like to be alone because you think that's what you deserve
You don't
You gravitate towards assholes who verify your belief that you should
be alone
They're wrong
Life is short and time betrays us all
Death comes from nowhere and taps us on the shoulder and says time to
go
Live while u can
Let go of what you think you are that's wrong
Love

It's raining

It's raining outside I can hear it

And that's ironic because it's raining in my heart as well

I'm so sad

And you're not allowed to say that when you're a man cause we're not
allowed to be sad it's the rules

Whose rules I don't know

Boy it's really coming down

I hear it trickling against my roof

And invading my porch

Boy I'm really sad

And worried

And hoping all this madness will be over one day

I worry about my daughters

1 is tough

And 1 is not

I just want them to be okay

Boy I'm really sad

Can you believe I'm saying that out loud?

There must be something wrong with me

All this brutal honesty

It's just not normal

Wear a mask so to speak

It will protect you so to speak

People will judge you and think you're weak

You can feel bad all you want

Just don't say it out loud

Boy I'm really sad

Pride and Prejudice
Sometimes I'm Mr. Darcy
Sometimes I'm Mr. Wickham

I'll be honest I'm both
You appear to be gone
I thought you were Elizabeth
Human love is so complicated
The enduring of it or the procurement
It's always a mess
Shakespeare was right the road to it is screwed
I think sometimes love wishes humans would leave it alone
Part ways with it so to speak
I'm
Inherently stupid because I'm a man
We don't know anything about love or what your gender wants
Or how to make you happy
We know how to piss you off and ruin things quite consistently and for
that I am sorry
Love must be tired of us
Like a violin played by someone who doesn't know how to play it

Séance
Channeling ghosts of the past on a daily basis
I can't let go
I can't move on
All my future hopes
Turn into my past regrets
You come to me offering the world and hope and love
And someone to wash dishes with
And to sit at the park with
I've been alone forever
I'm quite good at it
You never see two spiders in a web
If you do it's not for long
I thought it was you
But in the end you'll be someone I don't talk with anymore who love
almost became a thing
A brass ring I missed
A wedding ring I kissed
And put back in the box and returned to the jeweler
For a partial refund

Life guard
Swim ashore
To you
If you are their waiting
Floating in the water like a buoy
I can't move to be honest
The water is dark and cold
Like my heart
Would you rescue me?
Pull me from the deep
Back to dry land
Would you save me?
I need you too
Want you too
My arms are getting weak
And my legs can barely kick anymore
I just float here the best that I can
Living off of the fantasy that you love me
And we're okay and that
My second chance is real this time with you
I've never been in love before
This time it's real I know
I was a liar all of the rest
Or a fool

Hell maybe both

A Season in Hell

A season in hell I know so well for my life is a season in hell

I felt the devil crack my spine and drink my soul like slow red wine

Dark

Dark

All of the time

And the eyes of others are always blind

Made in the USA
Coppell, TX
20 June 2022

79056308R00121